TITANICA

IN MEMORY OF TITANIC HEROES

TITANICA

*The Disaster of the Century
in Poetry, Song, and Prose*

SELECTED, WITH A PREFACE BY

Steven Biel

W. W. NORTON & COMPANY
NEW YORK • LONDON

The text of this book is composed in Centaur
with the display set in Shelley Andante
Composition by ComCom
Manufacturing by The Haddon Craftsmen
Book design by JUDITH STAGNITTO ABBATE

Library of Congress Cataloging-in-Publication Data

Titanica : the disaster of the century in poetry, song, and prose /
    selected, with a preface by Steven Biel.
        p.   cm.
    ISBN 0-393-31873-7 (pbk.)
    I. Titanic (Steamship)—Literary collections.   2. Ship-
wrecks—Literary collections.   3. American literature—20th
century.   I. Biel, Steven, 1960– .
PS509.T57T58 1998
810.8'0358—dc2I   98-7986
                                                                CIP

W. W. Norton & Company, Inc., 500 Fifth Avenue
New York, N.Y. 10110
http://www.wwnorton.com

W. W. Norton & Company Ltd., 10 Coptic Street
London WC1A IPU

1 2 3 4 5 6 7 8 9 0

For Betsy Apple and Matt Brogan

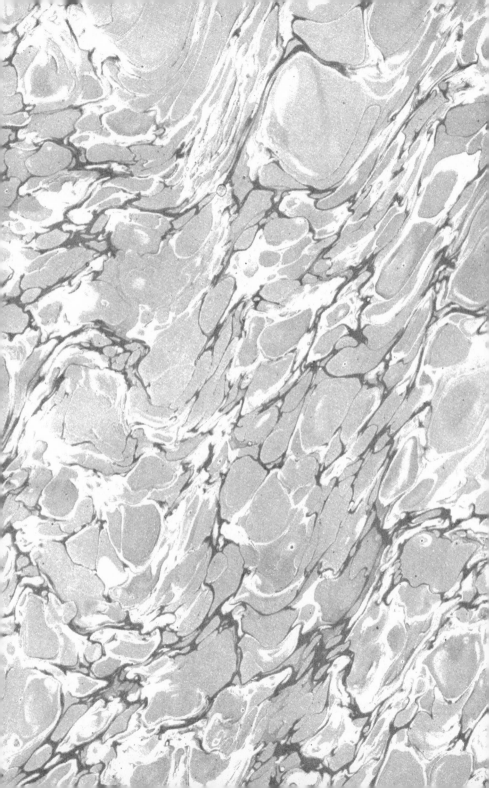

Contents

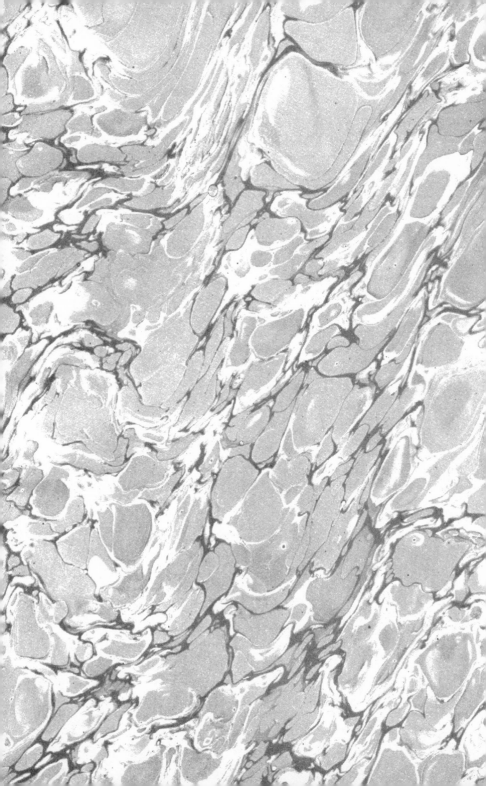

Preface

TWICE in the two weeks following the sinking of the *Titanic,* the *New York Times* warned against amateurs trying to write poems about the disaster. "No Subject for the Inexperienced," an editorial advised three days after the wreck. Twelve days later, with the new verses still coming in at a rate of dozens a day (down from hundreds in the first grief-stricken week), the *Times* felt compelled "to say again that to write about the Titanic a poem worth printing requires that the author should have something more than paper, pencil, and a strong feeling that the disaster was a terrible one." Most of the poems it had received were "worthless" and "intolerably bad"; the worst of all, the editors snobbishly complained, were written on lined paper.

The *Bookman* blamed America's literary elite, "always so mute on public affairs or current events," for writing "little or nothing" on the subject of the *Titanic,* while Britain's lions—including Thomas Hardy, Joseph Conrad, George Bernard Shaw, and Arthur Conan Doyle—publicly aired their views. *Current Literature,* which found Hardy's "The Convergence of the Twain" fine in conception but "very trying indeed" in execution, was kinder to America's aspiring *Titanic* bards: "We do not remember any other event in our history that has called forth such a rush of song in the columns of the daily press. Some of it has been unutterably bad and none of it has been what we would call magically inspired: yet there has been a very creditable amount of very creditable verse written on the subject."

Here is some of that very creditable verse—and very creditable writing of other kinds—along with some that really is intolerably, unutterably bad. None of it, though, is worthless. Across the years, its turgidness and unoriginality seem more poignant than irritating: reflections of a powerful impulse to make sense of the senseless, to recast the shocking and unknown in terms of the comfortable and known. If the *Titanic* disaster, which took 1,500 lives on the night of April 14 and the morning of April 15, 1912, could be fit into the familiar literary molds, maybe the horror could be transformed into something useful and good.

Here, too, are poems and song lyrics and prose excerpts that the *New York Times*, the *Bookman*, and *Current Literature* couldn't have found the adjectives to describe, couldn't have imagined: different ways of making sense of the disaster, vernacular interpretations far removed from the standards and expectations of the literary establishment. What would the publishers of "A Titan sailed her weary leagues of foam, / Unknowing her strange wish, her mad desire" (Charles Hanson Towne, "The Harvest of the Sea") possibly have thought of the spoken verses making the rounds of African-American communities: "He swimmed on till he came to a New York town, / and people asked had the Titanic gone down. / Shine said, 'Hell, yeah.' They said, 'How do you know?' / He said, 'I left the big motherfucker sinkin' about thirty minutes ago' "?

From the moment the first wireless messages reached shore, the *Titanic* became a metaphor, its meanings inseparable from the event itself. Actually, it became many metaphors, conflicting metaphors, each vying to define the disaster's broader social and political significance, to insist that *here* was the true meaning, the real lesson.

So, as a metaphor for divine judgment, the *Titanic* stirred up anxieties about greed, pride, and luxury. Was the disaster, with its heroic displays of Christian self-sacrifice, good news for morality, piety, and progress? Or was it a dire warning about the sinful state of modern souls?

As a metaphor for gender relations, the *Titanic* steamed into the debate over women's rights. Did "the rule of the sea"—"Women and Children First"—demonstrate that women were better off entrusting themselves to the protection of chivalrous men than trying to claim political power? Or did it prove that such disasters wouldn't happen when women voters, by demanding enlightened legislation, checked the avarice and stupidity that had caused the wreck?

As a metaphor for class relations, the *Titanic* crashed into the conflict between capital and labor. Did the heroism of the first-class men confirm the generosity and the natural superiority of the rich and powerful? Or were the stories of John Jacob Astor and the rest of the millionaire heroes a pack of lies concocted by the lackey commercial press? Were the real heroes the people down below in the steerage and the boiler room?

As a metaphor for race relations, the *Titanic* plunged into the racial divide. Was the conduct of the disaster's "Anglo-Saxon" heroes, who supposedly stayed calm and preserved order while swarthier people panicked, evidence of white supremacy? Or was the disaster the result of Anglo-Saxon arrogance and blundering? Were there African Americans on board? Were they heroes, too?

Everyone seemed to find ammunition in the *Titanic,* and only a few objected to the whole premise of using the tragedy to fight the battles of the day. In Maryland, a suffragist called it "a desecration to inject the question of woman suffrage into the *Titanic* disaster." Maybe it was a desecration. But maybe grief and sorrow alone weren't enough. Maybe politicizing the disaster—metaphorizing it—was the most genuine, the most human response. As Senator Isidor Rayner passionately explained, "I will not rehearse the agonies of this midnight sacrifice. I can not afford to dwell upon them or listen to the details that almost distract the mind and break the heart. It is the lesson and the moral that I am searching for."

At the end of the century, the *Titanic* has resurfaced as a pop-culture phenomenon. *Titanic*mania—a Tony-winning Broadway musical, a TV miniseries, documentaries, recordings, books, newspaper and magazine articles, museum exhibits, CD-ROMs, Web sites, and, of course, the Oscar-winning, record-breaking movie—reveals that the disaster speaks to us still.

Or speaks to us again, *in* time as much as *across* it, since the disaster's significance has undoubtedly changed over the years. Whatever meanings it may hold for us now—an all-purpose warning against our own faith in technology and progress? a general reminder of the value of self-sacrifice, civility, and decency? a vague hint of populist resentment bubbling just below the calm surface of American prosperity?—

pale against the complex and conflicting meanings that Americans gave to it in the months after the sinking. And no matter how obsessed we seem to be with the *Titanic*, nothing will ever compare to the way it haunted American culture in 1912.

STEVEN BIEL
May 1998

POEMS

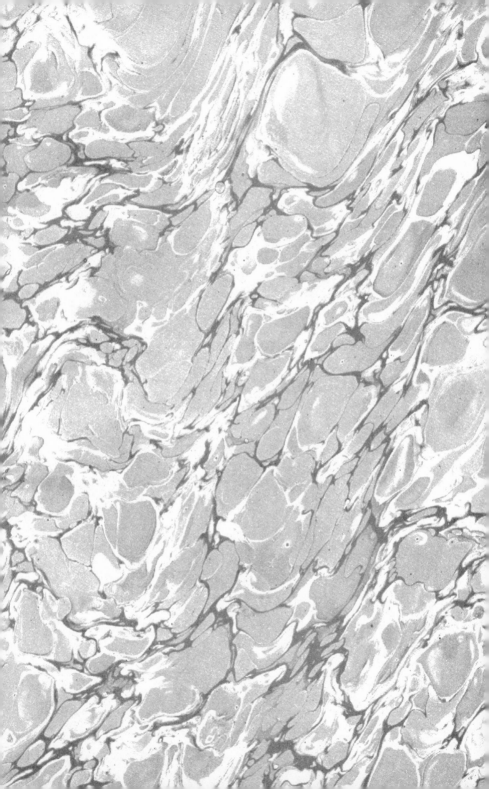

Fate's Comedy

THOMAS DOOLAN
1912

A thousand years since, Fate had planned
    To stage a playlet on the sea,
And moved her pawns with patient hand
    To build a merry comedy.

She caught the raindrops from the sky
    And welded them with icy blows,
Until they towered mountain high—
    An iceberg mid the Northland floes.

A thousand years have come and gone
    While men have slowly learned their part.
Each gave his little brain or brawn,
    That Fate might try her comic art.

Some burrowed deep in endless night,
    To break the steel from earth's strong grip,
While others forged the atoms bright
    And built for Fate a noble ship.

They pitted toil and ant-like skill
    Against the chance of Fate's grim game;
With hope to fright her cruel will,
    They gave their craft a giant's name.

And when the scene and stage were set,
    And all things tuned in time and space,
The puppet ship and iceberg met
    True in the long appointed place.

A little crash that scarce was heard
    Across the pulsing deep a mile,
A little cry, a frightened word,
    And Fate put on an age-worn smile.

The stars looked down in cold content,
    The waves rolled on their endless way,
And jaded Fate, her interest spent,
    Began to plot another play.

The Harvest of the Sea

CHARLES HANSON TOWNE (1877–1949)
Poet, Magazine Editor, Actor
1912

The jealous Sea moaned in the April night:
"Lo! there are comrades hidden in my heart,
Unfortunates who sought me, sick of life.
But I am hungry for brave souls; I crave
Their warmth and passion through my chilling tides;
Their heads upon my bosom, and their hands,
Like children's hands, about me in the dark.
I need their blood in my cold loneliness."

A Titan sailed her weary leagues of foam,
Unknowing her strange wish, her mad desire.
But there was menace in the starlit night,
And sudden doom upon deceiving paths,
And a wild horror on the mighty deep.

The grey Sea laughed—and drew those brave men down,
And braver women who but mocked at Death,
Seeing that Love went with them. These the souls
The awful Sea desired! These the hearts
She waited for in that stupendous hour!
They were enough to warm the Arctic wastes,
To fill with furnace heat the frozen zones,
And fire the very Sea that was their grave.

But dream not, mighty Ocean, they are yours!
We have them still, those high and valiant men
Who died that others might reach ports of peace.
Not in your jealous depths their spirits roam,
But through the world to-day, and up to heaven!

The Titanic

KATHARINE LEE BATES (1859–1929)
Poet, College Professor, Author of "America the Beautiful"
1912

As she sped from dawn to gloaming, a palace upon the sea,
Did the waves from her proud bows foaming whisper what port
  should be?
That her maiden voyage was tending to a haven hushed and deep,
Where after the shock and the rending she should moor at the wharf
  of sleep?

Oh, her name shall be tale and token to all the ships that sail,
How her mighty heart was broken by blow of a crystal flail,
How in majesty still peerless her helpless head she bowed
And in light and music, fearless, plunged to her purple shroud.

Did gleams and dreams half-heeded, while the days so lightly ran,
Awaken the glory seeded from God in the soul of man?
For touched with a shining chrism, with love's fine grace imbued,
Men turned them to heroism as it were but habitude.

O midnight strange and solemn, when the icebergs stood at gaze,
Death on one pallid column, to watch our human ways
And saw throned Death defeated by a greater lord than he,
Immortal Life, who greeted home-comers from the sea.

The Titanic

GEORGE A. HILL
Railroad Foreman
Mellenville, New York
1912

Steaming so swift and boldly
    Built so firm from keel to deck,
Thinking no power could daunt her,
    No wind, nor wave could wreck.

But deep down in their water pathway
    Lay that foe so cold and still,
To wreck that floating palace,
    And many hearts to ever still.

Little ones were made orphans,
    Widows and mothers left forlorn,
When those souls sank forever
    On that star-lit heavenly morn.

Fathers, mothers, brothers and sisters;
    Infants on their mothers' breasts
Were torn from one another
    To struggle and die in the foaming crest

Wives and husbands on the deck
    With a parting kiss said good-bye,
While many in love's tender embrace
    Remained in each other's arms to die.

Poverty and wealth went hand in hand;
    Side by side they sank.
God showed no distinction
    In station, creed or rank.

Then from that sinking deck
    A sweet melody waved o'er the lee
Between each shriek and groan
    "Nearer, My God, to Thee."

This proves how frail man doth build,
    And by it a lesson we are taught,
When compared with the work of God
    How quickly it is brought to naught.

Redeemed!

"THE BENTZTOWN BARD"
1912

They stand redeemed! They are not what we said,
Or felt, or thought; they are the kingly dead,
Who turned heroic after years of sloth
To save the weak. No longer need we loath
These rich whom slander oft has smeared with muck—

God tested them, and there they proved their pluck—
Young lovers parting at the gates of death
With one long, lingering kiss, one tender breath
Of immemorial greeting and farewell—
The lonely sea, and whither none could tell!

They stand redeemed, these idle sons that bore
The slurs and sneering of the world before!
In that great moment they were true, they stood
To help the helpless and forget the brood
Of selfish purpose that we said they nursed
In bosoms many have condemned and cursed:
They passed from honeymoons and dreams and tears
Beyond the multiple and blinding fears
Into the arms of ocean, giving up
Without one quiver—bravely—life's sweet cup!

They stand redeemed! These fathers, brothers, men!
They bring old faith in manhood back again.
Beside the boats they stood and saw dear wives
Take the one chance that in doom's hour survives—
The chance made possible by sacrifice
When manly men fold arms and pay the price
Of their own lives that those they love may live.
With all their wealth they gave what few would give—
Gave life and love and hope in stern deed
Sealed by Christ's love and deathless as His creed!

They stand redeemed! These volunteers of death,
These severed comrades, breathing still the breath
Of dews immortal where above them sweep
The waves that kiss and rock them to their sleep;
These "social monsters," judged aright at last
As burying bravely in that hour all cast,
All fine distinctions, pride and pedigree,
In wide-armed brotherhood of that vast sea
That clasps no nobler manhood than they knew
When Love and Death there tried and found them true!

They stand redeemed! Yea, it will matter not
How ill they lived when fortunate their lot.
In that dread hour they saw and knew the light,
They grew in manhood and they acted right,
Heroic manhood casting with its tide
All lesser traits they may have known aside:
Before the world that sorrows for them all
Who answered thus heroically the call,
They stand redeemed, the dead who greatly died
Purged by their deed of all their sin and pride!

They stand redeemed, these Titans of our day—
Husbands and wives who kissed and turned away;
Lovers and comrades on whom still the bloom
Of bridal sat with all its rare perfume;
Old hearts and young, twined hopes that severed there
In the black hour of sadness and despair;
Joy and adventure, laughter, sweetness, power—
Calm in that sudden and inviolate hour
Of new-born manhood to go down divine
In the great sea, forevermore its shrine!

     Today the world is all one part—
     A great, vast, sympathizing heart.

Brave men stood back that women might be saved,
But there were heroines, too—
Those wives who clung in death where danger waved
To all they loved so true.
No kiss farewell for them on lips that soon
Would leave them and go down,
But there together clasping death's sweet boon
They won immortal crown
Yea, there together on that doomed deck those,
Who proved that they were wed
To love forever, in that last hour chose
The nuptials of the dead!

No blame, no anger—not amid the gray
That wraps the earth in brotherhood today.

From *Titanic's Knell: A Satire on Speed*

HENRY BRENNER
St. Meinrad, Indiana
1932

O cruel frenzy
  Of modern progress,
   To allure her sons
    Into the net of Death,
All for the fame—
  So vain, so vain—
   Of such an empty name!

From *In Memoriam: The Titanic Disaster*

H. REA WOODMAN
Poughkeepsie, New York
1913

Impregnable Foe from the Arctic,
Drift on the uttermost sea!
On unfoughten deserts of ocean
The wrecks of your menace let be;

Insult the frail ships with your beauty,
Strike fierce with your dull hidden hate;
Serene from the innocent waters
Lift grandly your shoulders of state;

Summon your white powers of terror
To garner the havoc you crave,
But sore in your memory shall rankle
The thought of that triumphant grave;

How bitter soever your scourging
Of the man-driven sea you hate,
For aye shall you hear the bold music
Of the dying before the Gate;

How bitter soever the knowing,
It shall come or early or late:
Your vengeance was robbed of its potence
By that singing before the Gate.

The Convergence of the Twain

THOMAS HARDY (1840–1928)
Author
1912

In a solitude of the sea,
Deep from human vanity,
And the Pride of Life that planned her, stilly couches she.

Steel chambers, late the pyres
Of her salamandrine fires,
Cold currents thrid and turn to rhythmic tidal lyres.

Over the mirrors meant
To glass the opulent,
The sea-worm crawls—grotesque, slimed, dumb, indifferent.

Jewels in joy designed
To ravish the sensuous mind
Lie lightless, all their sparkles bleared and black and blind.

Dim moon-eyed fishes near
The daintly gilded gear
Gaze querying: "What does all this sumptuousness down here?"

Well: while was fashioning
This ship of swiftest wing,
The Immanent Will, that stirs and urges everything,

Prepared a sinister Mate
For her—so gaily great—
A Shape of Ice, for the time far and dissociate.

And as the smart ship grew
In stature, grace and hue,
In shadowy silent distance grew the Iceberg, too.

Alien they seemed to be:
No mortal eye could see
The intimate welding of their later history,

Or sign that they were bent
By paths coincident
On being anon twin halves of one august event;

Till the Spinner of the Years
Said "Now!" The which each hears,
And consummation comes, and jars two hemispheres.

Fair Play

M. L. CLAWSON
1912

A monument for millionaires
A monument for snobs.
No marble shaft for the men on the craft,
Who simply worked at their jobs.

The owner of gold and the wearer of lace
Is the thing that determines a hero's place.
But I'll sing a song to right the wrong,
I'll sing of the loyal crew.

In the hold of the ship, who never knew
How the hand of death did fall
Of the band that played while the good ship swayed
Unmindful of the call.

I'll drop a tear to the boys in the hold,
Who never knew and never were told
Who lived alone by the engine's throbs
And died as they lived—at work on their jobs.

I'll speak a word and breathe a prayer,
For those now drifting with the tide
Here's a cheer, and a sob
And a tear o'er their ocean bier
To the men who died with their jobs.

Enough Said

CLARK MCADAMS (1874–1935)
Journalist, Newspaper Editor
1912

"Votes for women!"
Was the cry,
Reaching upward
To the sky.
Crashing glass,
And flashing eye—
"Votes for women!"
Was the cry.

"Boats for women!"
Was the cry,

When the brave
Were come to die.
When the end
Was drawing nigh—
"Boats for women!"
Was the cry.

Life has many
Little jests
Insignificant
As tests.
Doubt and bitterness
Assail
But "Boats for women!"
Tells the tale.

A Requiem

HARRIET MONROE (1860–1936)
Founder and Editor of Poetry: A Magazine of Verse
1912

Sleep softly in your ocean bed,
Ye brave who dared to die!
Your fathers, who at Shiloh bled,
Accept your company.

Ye sons of warriors, lightly rest—
Daughters of pioneers!
Heroes freeborn, who chose the best,
Not tears for you, but cheers!

Lovers of life, who life could give,
Sleep softly where ye lie!
Ours be the vigil! Help us live,
Who teach us how to die.

From *The Titanic Disaster Poem*

J. H. McKenzie
Guthrie, Oklahoma
1912

And Strauss,* who did the children feed,
    Had mercy on the poor,
And all such men the world doth need
    To reverence evermore.
Oh, may the union of Strauss and wife
    Be memorial to all men,
Each for the other gave their life,
    A life we should commend;
And may all the girls who chance in life
    To read this poem thru
Emulate the deed of such a wife,
    As went down in the blue.

The Titanic

Corinne Roosevelt Robinson (1861–1933)
Reformer, Poet, Author of My Brother, Theodore Roosevelt
1912

Parting

BELOVED, you must go—ask not to stay,
    You are a mother and your duties call;
    And we, who have so long been all in all,
Must put the human side of life away.

---

*First-cabin passengers Isidor and Ida Straus stayed together to die on the *Titanic.*
Isidor, founder of Macy's Department Store, was a celebrated philanthropist.

For one brief moment let us stand and pray,
    Sealed in the thought that whatsoe'er befall
    We, who have known the freedom and the thrall
Of a great love, in death shall feel its sway.—
You, who must live, because of his dear need,
You are the one to bear the harder part;—
Nay, do not cling—'tis time to say good-by.
Think of me then but as a spirit freed—
Flesh of my Flesh, and Heart of my own Heart
The love we knew has made me strong to die.

TOGETHER

I CANNOT leave you, ask me not to go,
    Love of my youth and all my older years;
    We, who have met together many smiles or tears,
Feeling that each did but make closer grow
The union of our hearts— Ah! say not so
    That Death shall find us separate. All my fears
    Are but to lose you. Life itself appears
A trifling thing— But one great truth I know,
When heart to heart has been so closely knit
That Flesh has been one Flesh and Soul one Soul,
Life is not life if they are rent apart—
And death unsevered is more exquisite,
As we, who have known much, shall read the whole
Of Life's great secret on each other's heart!

The Titanic

BRAND WHITLOCK (1869–1934)
Republican Mayor of Toledo, Ohio, Diplomat, Author
1912

"And this," the dark Ironic Spirit mocked
As it beheld the proud new lofty ship

Upon its westering way across the sea,
"This is thy latest, greatest miracle,
The triumph of thy science, art and all
That skill thou'st learnt since forth the Norsemen fared
Across these waters in their cockle shells,
In dodging back and forth 'twixt storm and sea,
Until at last, in this thy master work,
Thou'dst go in safety and in pride, and boast
Meanwhile of thine unparalleled achievement,
Thy victory o'er my wanton will and whim!
Ho, Little Man, behold! I'd not waste e'en
A tempest on thy paragon, but thus,
Upon its first glad, confident adventure,
With but a cast-off fragment of my store
Of power—thus to the bottom of the seas
For evermore, with this thy latest marvel
And with thee! Ho! Ho!"
                    The awful laugh
Rang through the dreadful reaches of the Void.
But lo! The calm and all-sufficient answer
Of our intrepid Northern race! With lips
Drawn tight, they look with clear, dry eyes on doom,
And so confront the end, there in the night
That was to have for them no pitying dawn.
(Their kind alone of all intelligence
Feels pity.)
                    "The women and the children first.
We stay."
                    No cry, no whimpering; and there,
Up there, upon the dark, mysterious bridge,
The grizzled captain, chief of all those victims
Of Its sublime, stupendous, bitter joke,
But the exemplar of that race which knows
How to aspire, achieve, and dare Its wrath,
And in the hour of failure, how to die.

Titanic Toast

Version from Otey, Texas
Recorded in 1965

It was sad indeed, it was sad in mind,
April the 14th of 1912 was a hell of a time,
when the news reached a seaport town
that the great Titanic was a sinking down.
Up popped Shine from the deck below,
says, "Captain, captain," says, "you don't know."
Says, "There's about forty feet of water on the boiler room floor."
He said, "Never mind, Shine, you go on back, and keep stackin' them
    sacks,
I got forty-eight pumps to keep the water back."
Shine said, "Well, that seems damned funny, it may be damned fine,
but I'm gonna try to save this black ass of mine."
So Shine jumped overboard and begin to swim,
and all the people standin' on deck watchin' him.
Captain's daughter ran on the deck with her dress above her head and
    her titties below her knees,
and said, "Shine, Shine, won't you save poor me?"
Say, "I'll make you as rich as any shine can be."
Shine said, "Miss, I know you is pretty and that is true,
but there's women on the shore can make a ass out a you."
So Shine turned over and began to swim,
people on the deck were still watchin' him.
A whale jumped up in the middle of the sea,
said, "Put a 'special delivery' on his black ass for me."
Shine said, "Your eyes may roll and your teeth may grit,
but if you're figurin' on eatin' me you can can that shit."
Shine continued to swim, he looked back, he ducked his head, he
    showed his ass,
"Look out sharks and fishes and let me pass."
He swimmed on till he came to a New York town,
and people asked had the Titanic gone down.

Shine said, "Hell, yeah." They said, "How do you know?"
He said, "I left the big motherfucker sinkin' about thirty minutes
   ago."

The "Titanic"

M. C. LEHR

Within the dungeon of the deep
   There sleeps the queen of all the seas,
Who swung assurance at the sweep
   Of ghostly peril on the breeze,
And dared the elements to ply
   Their angered forces at her head
That she might battle and defy—
   And lo! *one* battle left her dead!

With all the graces of a court
   She slipped the tethers of the tide
And glided far from out the port
   That bound her power and her pride;
And with the promise of her youth
   And all the future in her sway,
She strode in triumph over truth
   And tossed the danger with the spray!

Within, her heart was great and gay,
   Without, her sinews stretched in length,
The very heavens seemed to play
   Beside the pulses of her strength!
And through the day and through the night
   Of billowed pleasure undismayed,
Her throb of fervor set to flight
   The toll of fear, and fear obeyed.

Peace! While the even waters glide
    By quiet stars from night to day;
Peace! While the measured hours stride
    In swift descent upon their prey;
And there in shrouded silence steals
    The stealthy espion of the sea,
Whose frozen mask afar conceals
    The dark decree of destiny.

Peace! While the miracle of man
    Yet flies her flag in majesty;
Peace! While she breathes her final span
    Serene unto eternity;
And then—the muffled knell of doom,
    The flash of fate, the riven rod,
The plunge into the gulf of gloom,
    And last—the very touch of God!

A thousand lives embosomed are
    Beneath the wonders of the wave,
A thousand spirits vanished far
    Beyond the waters of the grave;
And sunken in that solemn keep,
    The carcass of a vessel vast,
Where only weeds and fishes creep
    Among the port-holes of the past!

No marble monolith may mark,
    Brave sons! the traces of your doom,
Where but the caverns of the shark
    Return the echoes of the tomb,
And but a broken bulk of steel
    Crushed in the sea's eternal bed,
Shall tell the distant ages still
    Where tender homage may be led.

And yet, about that shattered shell
    Whose glory crumbled in an hour,

The waves may wind a coral spell
   And weave a poem into power,
Until the heaving depths of slime
   And clinging beauties of the deep
Shall mold a monument sublime
   Unto your ceremented sleep.

And here, since every sorrow swings
   Some note of beauty on the tide,
And not a dark despair but brings
   A feeble glimmer to abide,
Bereaved, benumbed, all hearts may fold
   About the courage of the dead,
And honor strength that died enrolled
   To yield the weaker, life instead.

And while the winds and waters merge
   In mournful requiem of sighs,
And chant a great eternal dirge
   Of far regret unto the skies,
The wave of all the ages still
   Shall sweep the reef of memory,
And yearning breakers curve and thrill
   In music of your eulogy!

O Sea!

LUCIAN B. WATKINS (1879–1921)
Poet, Teacher
1912

O Sea! O Sea! O Sea!
   Ah, raving hungry Sea!
When wilt thy heartless greed be satisfied,
Or wilt thy cruel craving be supplied
   With earth's humanity!

Stay thou, O Sea, thy long and mighty arm,
    That icy, icy arm,
    That awful, awful arm
       That sweeps so far that we
Must ever shudder with the sense of harm,
Must feel and fear with merciless alarm
    The cold embrace of thee!

When rocking on the bosom of thy wave,
    Thy rippling, rolling wave,
    Thy swinging surging wave,
      We rest in ecstasy,
Mar not the dreams of happiness we crave,
Ope not thy deep and dark abysmal grave
    To seal our destiny!

Oh, spare us from yon tragic spectre there,
    That grewsome spectre there;
    That deadly spectre there
      Where the Titanic be!
Dear hearts there to baptism did repair
In this the soul's triumphant hour of prayer,
    In true nobility!

Lo! who are those great beings over there,
    Those toiling figures there,
    Those smiling faces there
      'Mid death and misery?
They're heroes kissing babes and women fair
Farewell for homes they ne'er with them can share
    Again beyond the sea!

O ye sea-gulls that wing about the scene,
    This dreadful sorrow scene,
    This martyr-crimson scene
      Of saddest memory,
Beneath these briny waters blue and green
Lie wealth and rags alike and all they mean
    Waiting eternity!

Lord God! when man had made the biggest boat,
 The best and grandest boat,
 The fastest moving boat
  That e'er the world did see,
A golden palace on the sea afloat,
The thing on which his dearest pride did dote,
 All was but vanity!

 O Sea! O Sea! O Sea!
 Ah, raving hungry Sea!
When wilt thy heartless greed be satisfied,
Or wilt thy cruel craving be supplied
 With earth's humanity!

The Titanic Pigmy

ROBERT HUGH MORRIS (1876–1942)
Minister
1912

Lord, we have boasted we are wise;
 We comb the clouds with surcharged wires,
 And borrow their electric fires—
We snatch our message from the skies.

And, Lord, we boasted we are strong;
 Our ships we build of fire-tried steel,
 A million rivets bind the keel—
Two million more the hulk along.

We boasted, Lord, that we are swift;
 We shoot like sea-birds o'er the waves
 No matter how the wind behaves,
And into port we calmly drift.

And lo! this warning from the sea
    That wisdom is but loaned to man,
    And that since first the world began
All might and power belong to Thee.

Swift are our titans; swifter far
    Than twinkling eye or quick-caught breath
    That messenger whom we call death
Comes riding in his noiseless car.

Great God, teach us to boast no more;
    We have no wisdom and no might—
    We are but pilgrims of a night
And trav'lers to the unseen shore.

SERMONS *and*

THE WAS A MAN

BRAVERY

HEROES & CHILDREN FIRST

HEROES

HENRY B.

HERO

COL ASTOR

HEROES

THE MARINE BAND

HERO

HEROES

SAILORS

MAJOR BUTT

SELF-SACRIFICE

TOLL FOR THE BRAVE! —
THE BRAVE THAT ARE NO MORE!
ALL SUNK BENEATH THE WAVE
FAST BY THEIR NATIVE SHORE!
COWPER

THE GUARDIAN ANGEL OF THE SEA PAYS TRIBUTE TO THE MARTYRED HEROES

RELIGIOUS VIEWS

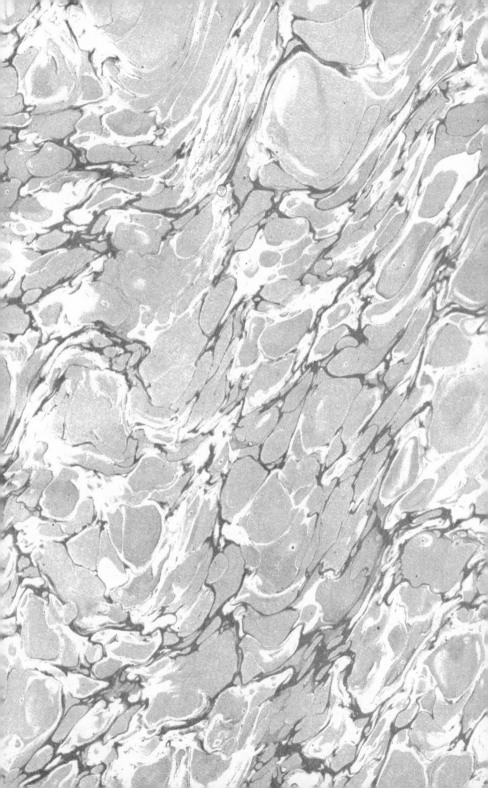

From a Sermon, Madison Avenue Presbyterian Church, New York

REVEREND CHARLES H. PARKHURST (1842–1933)
Minister, Reformer
April 21, 1912

I have used the event of the sinking of the Titanic because it is tremendously in the general mind at the moment and on the public nerve, and because it is the terrific and ghastly illustration of what things come to when men throw God out at the door and take a golden calf in at the window.

I have used it because it exhibits on a monstrous scale that everything is for existence and nothing for life, and that everything lends an ear to the hard, cold, glittering metallic basis of the dollar. I am impelled to this not by any motive of anger, but by indignation that is hot and holy.

For all this sorrow, this horrible slaughter, this parting of loved ones, tragic rending of families, separation of husbands and wives, fathers and children, lovers and brides, at the moment of the ship's immersion, was totally without reason.

This last week, since Tuesday morning, has been a serious one—

serious not only for the bereaved, but serious for the city, the country, and the world. The very complexion of the town has altered itself. The public has been imaginatively the witness of an appalling tragedy. We have been sobered by it, for it has cut down into the very fabric of our souls. We have been shaken by it, for it has pierced us to a point deeper than where we ordinarily live. It has bored down into the substrata of our being.

Different temperaments have, of course, seized upon different aspects of this unparalleled tragedy. Each of you has your own line of contemplation. I am going to tell you mine, and I am going to cut as close to the line of truth and to the nerve of the sensitive heart as I know how; for if this event is treated as it ought to be it is going to produce some searchings of heart that will modify to a degree the attitude of the general mind toward certain vital questions of individual and public life.

The picture which presents itself before my eyes is that of the glassy, glaring eyes of the victims, staring meaninglessly at the gilded furnishings of this sunken palace of the sea; dead helplessness wrapped in priceless luxury; jewels valued in seven figures becoming the strange playthings of the queer creatures that sport in the dark depths. Everything for existence, nothing for life. Grand men, charming women, beautiful babies, all becoming horrible in the midst of the glittering splendor of a $10,000,000 casket!

And there was no need of it. It is just so much sacrifice laid upon the accursed altar of the dollar. The boat had no business to be running in that lane. They knew that the ice was there. They dared it. They would dare it now were it not for the public. It is cheaper to run by the short route. There is more money in it for the stockholders. The multi-millionaires want more money. They want as much as they can get of it. The coal is now saved. It is starting a little mine at the bottom of the ocean between Sable Island and Cape Race.

It is a lesson all around to the effect that commercialism, when pushed beyond a certain pace, breaks down and results in stringency and poverty; and that action, when crowded, produces reaction that wipes out the results of action.

And then there is the matter of the insufficiency of lifeboats. I recall now what a Captain on an ocean liner said to me twenty years ago.

We were standing on the deck, and he admitted then that his ship had insufficient lifeboats to save all in case of accident.

"What would you do if the ship were sinking?" I asked him.

"We would take off as many as we could and land them," he replied. Then he continued, with a fiendish chuckle, "And then we'd come back for the rest."

This cruel Captain's words have been repeated often since. But those boats that landed last Thursday night did not go back for the rest. Those that remained will stay there. The steamship companies want payment for what they carry. Lifeboats and rafts don't pay dividends. Passengers do. And they pay in advance and the money is in the treasury, ready to be divided as dividends.

Demands for improvements are always treated the same way. If neither Government nor the people demanded them the steamship companies would furnish lifeboats if the individual members of these companies—stanch, wealthy, godly men, most of them—thought as much of the value of human life as they do of what they receive in passage money. Willing to risk loss of life rather than diminish net gains! More commercialism! Lives against ducats! More worship of the golden calf! Worshipping God in the sanctuary and worshipping Mammon in the steamship business!

We can conceive no severer punishment for those steamship men—the one who is here now with the others*—than to be compelled to read and reread the harrowing details of those two hours from midnight to 2 A.M. on the morning of the sinking of the ship. We will not be angry with them. Rather will we pity them, for if their hearts have not been hardened to the consistency of the metal in which they deal, the perusal of the ghastly record, the contemplation of the vivid drama of men leaping to their death, bidding long good-byes to those loved ones, and all to the accompaniment of the infernal music of the orchestra, ought to give them a foretaste of the tortures of the damned.

Yes, we pity them, for unless their hearts are clean gone and burnt

---

*J. Bruce Ismay, Managing Director of the White Star Line, escaped the wreck in a lifeboat.

to a crisp these days are to them days of remorse, of gnawing of the soul. Their guilt is not momentary. It is driven home with a gold hammer, which will beat them into sensibility. Had Providence held back the tragedy the moral lesson only would have been delayed.

The two sore spots which really run into one another and which constitute the disease that is gnawing into our civilization are love of money and passion for luxury. Those two combined are what sunk the Titanic and sent 1,500 souls prematurely to their final account.

The passengers wanted to cross the Atlantic in a palace, and in order to satisfy them and win the spoils that would come by satisfying them, the ship management ordered the construction of a boat that would sacrifice the safety of passengers to the gratification of their tastes.

Then they ran the boat in a latitude, at a rate of speed, and under conditions of peculiar danger—all to gratify that silly passion for haste that comes with money and with the love of money.

The boat went plowing through the sea at the rate of 21½ knots an hour, with the Captain off the bridge and banqueting down in the salon, we are informed, in company with the official head of the line. That is the entire story. Money was the fundamental factor in the entire business.

There is one spot of brightness, only one. It puts a goodly touch of glory on the sinking Titanic that magnanimity, which is wont to slumber in every human soul, awakened and caused such a demonstration as we have seen for the last few days. Chivalrous death is better than cowardly living.

From a Speech on the Senate Floor

ISIDOR RAYNER (1850–1912)
Democratic Senator from Maryland
May 28, 1912

There is another lesson, however, Mr. President, that this disaster has taught us, of more importance than a change in our admiralty and navigation laws, and of far greater and more overwhelming significance than the lesson of corporate responsibility, and that is the lesson of religious faith. Disasters like this, instead of weakening, should strengthen the faith of the Nation. There is no use of appealing to reason or to philosophy in a case of this sort. The mind stands aghast and appalled as these calamities come thick and fast. We forget in our moments of sorrow that it never was intended that the intellect of man should reason out such a problem. Suffering and affliction, as they come to the pure and the innocent in a hundred forms, are inexplainable.

The convulsions of nature alone that have swept myriads of human beings to an untimely death can not be reconciled by any process of human reasoning. When reason halts, the Creator has implanted in the soul another faculty, however, that gives us light in the hours of tribulation. It is the light of faith, a pillar of fire in the night of our darkness and despair. Throughout my life I have spent many hours of the day, and many silent and sleepless hours of the night, in the struggle for the light of reason, but in my advancing years the light that gives me fortitude and courage is the sublime light of faith, that never dims nor wanes, and at the supreme moment when reason vanishes, breaks in upon us with all the radiance of the morning sun. We can reason out the negligence of man, but we can not reason out why, in the course of nature, an iceberg from the Arctic Zone should just at this very moment have taken its course upon the path of desolation and of death. Upon all this and kindred subjects the most profound intellect of the greatest philosophers who ever lived have illumined the world just about as much as the credulity of the earliest races who attributed every phenomenon of nature to the interposition of Divine Providence. What this Nation needs are some severe lessons that will strengthen the pillars and the altars of its faith. We are to a large extent to-day defying the ordinances of God, and the sooner we awaken to a realizing sense of our responsibility the better it will be for the spiritual elevation of the country. We are running mad with the lust of wealth, and of power, and of ambition. We are separating society into casts, with fabulous fortunes upon the one side and destitution and poverty on the other. It takes a terrible warning to bring us back to our moorings and our senses. We are abandoning the devout and simple lives of our ancestors, and the fabric of our firesides is weakening at the foundation. If this disaster teaches no lesson or points no moral, then let us pass it by with stoical indifference, until the next disaster comes, and in the meantime let the carnival go on. May the heart-rending scenes upon this night of anguish and of woe give us faith and lead us back to the altars of our fathers. I will not rehearse the agonies of this midnight sacrifice. I can not afford to dwell upon them or listen to the details that almost distract the mind and break the heart. It is the lesson and the moral that I am searching for.

I will say this, however, in closing: The agonies of separation at this scene, that palsy the tongue when it attempts to describe them, were worse than the agonies of death. I knew well one of the courageous passengers who, with his wife, yielded up their lives on this occasion.* The man was a splendid type of American citizenship. I served with him in the House of Representatives, and he was esteemed and beloved by all who knew him. In private life he was a benefactor of the human race. In public life he was an unpurchasable tribune of the people. His heroic wife had the blood of martyrs in her veins, and from the most authentic account that I can obtain, the account of a witness who was not examined by the committee, because her testimony was not necessary for the purposes of the investigation, she went to her death with the same spirit of heroic fortitude with which her ancestors went to the fagot and the flame.

A harrowing thought flashes across my mind, and that is, it might possibly have been unnecessary to have presented to this devoted man and woman the terrible alternative that confronted them, and it might have been possible that both of them could have been rescued. I shall dwell upon this incident no longer.

I shall close my brief remarks with this remembrance. As the ship was sinking the strains of music were wafted over the deck. It was not the note of any martial anthem that had in days gone by led embattled legions on to victory. It was a more inspiring stanza than this. It was a loftier and holier melody amid the anguish and the sublime pathos of that awful hour that swept through the compartments of the sinking ship. It was a rallying cry for the living and the dying—to rally them not for life, but to rally them for their awaiting death. Almost face to

*Isidor and Ida Straus.

face with their Creator, amid the chaos of this supreme and solemn moment, in inspiring notes the unison resounded through the ship. It told the victims of the wreck that there was another world beyond the seas, free from the agony of pain, and, though with somber tones, it cheered them on to their untimely fate. As the sea closed upon the heroic dead, let us feel that the heavens opened to the lives that were prepared to enter.

Father of the Universe, what an admonition to the Nation! The sounds of that awe-inspiring requiem that vibrated o'er the ocean have been drowned in the waters of the deep, the instruments that gave them birth are silenced as the harps were silenced on the willow tree, but if the melody that was rehearsed could only reverberate through this land, "Nearer, My God, to Thee," and its echoes could be heard in these halls of legislation, and at every place where our rulers and representatives pass judgment and enact and administer laws, and at every home and fireside, from the mansions of the rich to the huts and hovels of the poor, and if we could be made to feel that there is a divine law of obedience and of adjustment and of compensation that should command our allegiance, far above the laws that we formulate in this presence, then, from the gloom of these fearful hours we shall pass into the dawn of a higher service and of a better day, and then, Mr. President, the lives that went down upon this fated night did not go down in vain.

"S. O. S.—Save Our Souls," Sermon, Central Universalist Church, Indianapolis

REVEREND FRANK DURWARD ADAMS (1876–1962)
May 1912

I fancy I can see her as she sails triumphantly along, the greatest ship ever built by the hand of man. Overhead twinkle the stars in a cloudless sky. Below the restless sea, almost without a ripple, calm as an inland lake, except for the waves thrown up by the mighty leviathan as she ploughs her thrilling way through the waters.

On board there is music, joy and laughter. Some have retired to rest, others stroll upon the decks, or chat in the lounging rooms. And the splendid ship goes hurling through the waters at a speed of thirty miles an hour.

Then there is a cry of warning, three bells, danger dead ahead, a shock, a quiver in every fiber of the vessel, and a long moment of breathless silence. Surprise, anxiety and fear sweep over twenty-five hundred souls. Men, women and children come crowding out upon the decks, floods of cold sea water pour through a great rent in the side of the ship, and a grim, massive, mocking iceberg moves silently, irresistibly away. Now there is a call for the life-boats. Life-belts are brought out and distributed. "Women and children first," is the stern command, enforced if need be by the flaming pistol, as the boats are filled and hurriedly lowered over the side. And in the little room where the instruments are the brave Jack Phillips, his steady hand on the key, pounds out incessantly the distress call of the sea, "S. O. S., S. O. S., Save our souls! Save our souls!"*

The music has started up again, light opera, rag-time, the popular songs of the day. The heroic musicians are doing their best to prevent a panic. But the ship sinks lower and lower toward the water line. The life-boats, with their seven hundred souls, push away, leaving more than sixteen hundred to meet their certain doom. The bow plunges beneath the waves, there is a muffled explosion, and hundreds of men are seen leaping from the decks. Deck by deck the lights go out, the huge stern rises high in the air, and still the heart-breaking cry from the wireless, "Save our souls! Save our souls!"

The orchestra is still playing, but it's different music now. Hundreds of men on the doomed ship fall to their knees and lift their voices in broken song as the strains of "Nearer, My God, to Thee," come from the faltering instruments and even the wretched women in the boats make a feeble attempt to join in the hymn. Then the last of the lights go out, another muffled explosion as the bulkheads give way, and the beautiful Titanic, monarch of the seas, slips noiselessly beneath the waves.

---

*Jack Phillips, one of the *Titanic*'s wireless operators, used the distress signal "S. O. S." for the first time in history at the urging of his colleague, Harold Bride.

For one terrible minute there is silence. Then the air is rent with shrieks and groans and cries to God for help as the victims rise to the surface. Those in the boats thrust their fingers in their ears to shut out the cries, for they realize their pitiable inability to extend a helping hand. But even the groans and prayers die away little by little, and there is only the awful lonely silence of the sea. Men and women pull with benumbed hands and stony hearts at the oars, and the boats float out into the darkness, while 30, 25, 20 miles away the noble Carpathia, steaming heedless of her own danger at eighteen knots an hour, is speeding to the rescue.

There is no sound save the feeble dipping of the oars, the lapping of the waves against the life-boats, the muffled commands of the boats' captains, and the occasional cry of a widowed wife or a motherless child. Down in the depths of the sea, or floating stark upon its cold bosom, are 1,635 human bodies from whom life has forever fled, the great ship lies at the bottom of the ocean, and above in the heavens smile the stars, "The forget-me-nots of the angels."

I

THE PSYCHOLOGY OF THE DISASTER

Yes, it was a terrible tragedy. For days after it had happened it haunted me like a dreadful nightmare. Sleeping or waking I seemed to see the Titanic plunging, or about to plunge, into the waters with its helpless human freight. Yet, now, after a lapse of weeks, we are minded to wonder why it has gripped and thrilled and sickened us so.

The reasons are almost wholly psychological. All the circumstances were such as to appeal to the imagination; and wherever imagination holds sway there a profound impression is made. The **suddenness** of the tragedy strikes us. Nothing could be more unexpected. The sea was smooth, there was no wind, the sky was cloudless, the stars were shining. A few knew of the presence of ice near-by, but the passengers and crew were in blissful ignorance of danger. The traditional lightning out of a clear sky could not have created more consternation.

Besides being sudden, it was on a **tremendously big scale**. It was the greatest ship ever built by man; it was making a record voyage across the Atlantic; it had on board a list of passengers whose names sounded like a page torn from "Who's Who in America." Nobody thought the ship could sink, but when she went down she carried with her the largest number of victims ever lost in a disaster at sea. Everything about it was on a regular 20th century scale; and that means the greatest scale that history affords.

And how **dramatic** it was! If all the world is a stage, there was tragedy at its highest possible tension. Characters of world-wide reputation were on the stage. No master of pen or brush could have conceived such a setting—the greatest ship in all the world, sinking in two miles of water, two thousand human souls in jeopardy, the band playing, men and women performing deeds of heroism, farewells being spoken, lifeboats putting out to sea, the mocking mountain of ice slowly withdrawing into the night, and five hundred miles of open sea on every hand. Dramatic! The world has never seen the like in all the ages.

Then there is another reason, which to me at least, overshadows all the rest. That is the **absolute helplessness** of the victims. There was nothing they could do to save themselves. Above were the heavens, but they could not fly; below the icy waters, but it were idle to swim. Like all the world, they thought the Titanic could not sink; but when they saw her actually taking the fatal plunge they could only clutch at the empty air, and pray. Jack Phillips' frantic call, "Save our souls!" was but the echo of the wail that went up from 1,600 human souls staring full into the face of death, and with none to save.

That is why it has made such an appeal to our hearts. It was a sudden, great, dramatic, hopeless situation; and though the vividness of the picture fades as time passes, it will not be effaced from our minds while we live.

II

THINGS THAT ARE WORSE

But there can be no better time than right now, while the tension of this tragedy is still upon us, to recognize that there are many conditions, some of them under our very noses, a great deal worse than this, though they do not make the same appeal to our imaginations. The terrible **mine disasters,** that have occurred with heart-sickening frequency during the past two years or so, are immeasureably worse. And the toll of death has been much heavier. If I had to take my choice between death from suffocation by smoke, dust or gas in a mine explosion, down in the rayless depths of the bowels of the earth, and death by drowning in the clear, cold water of the Atlantic, under the stars, I'd take drowning every time. Wouldn't you? Yet there has been no such universal outcry over mine disasters, which are due, as we shall presently see, to exactly the same cause that sent the Titanic to the bottom.

About a year ago occurred the ghastly fire in the Triangle Shirt-Waist Factory, in New York City. Away up on the tenth floor of a skyscraper, with no fire-escapes worthy the name, the exits all locked, and every means of escape cut off, 150 young women and girls were roasted to death or dashed to unrecognizable pulp when they leaped from the tenth-story windows. Wouldn't you a thousand times rather see your mother, wife, sister or daughter go down to death with the queen of the ocean than roasted to death like a rat in a trap? I would. Yet the Triangle fire, due to exactly the same cause, thrilled a small part of the nation a part of one day, though it was a hundred times more terrible than the foundering of a ship.

CHILD LABOR

Every day of the world, twelve, fifteen, eighteen hours of the day, society faces the grim tragedy of **child-labor.** We see, not a few hundred doomed to a few minutes of death agony, but millions of little children chained without hope of release to the pitiless wheels of industry, while everything of beauty and worth is ground out of their poor lives forever. At the time of life when they should be playing in the sunshine, busy in the schoolroom, and developing physical, mental and moral power for the work of manhood and womanhood, they are kept at their tasks till the light leaves the eye, the color the cheeks, the buoyancy the step, and hope flees the heart. They rise from their poor beds at the break of day, snatch a bite of breakfast, and hurry off to work. They toil till the day is done, hurry back to the place they call home, eat a bit of supper, and drop into bed to sleep the sleep of utter exhaustion till the pitiless whistle calls them again to their task. Beside such lingering, leering murder, death in the ocean waters is tender mercy. Yet there is no universal outcry against this installment-murder of innocent childhood. The newspapers are not featuring it; there are no spectacular memorial services in memory of the helpless dead; no great relief funds, no Senatorial investigations. But the victims outnumber a thousand to one those who went down on the Titanic.

400 FEMALE VICTIMS EACH DAY

Just now the mayor of our city is much disturbed in mind as to what he shall do with the immoral houses and their inmates. Wellmeaning men and women, religious men and women, are demanding that he shall do something to close up these places. But few, if any of them, or the mayor himself, so far as I can discover, seem to understand that the same merciless power that hurled the Titanic to the bottom of the sea and 1,600 souls into eternity is the identical power that feeds and fattens upon prostitution and the white-slave traffic. Or, if they do, none of the remedies proposed would indicate it. They rightly talk about the fate of the poor victims now concerned, but not a word about shutting off the supply.

And who is wrought up over this gigantic curse? The papers, if they were inclined to feature it, would be hushed up by prudery and certain other powerful influences. Congress had an investigation made once, but the report was suppressed as unfit for publication. But, talk about ocean disasters! It would take **a hundred Titanic wrecks every year** to equal the sacrifice demanded annually by this leering god of lust and greed! Do you get the force of that statement? I will say it again. **It would take a hundred Titanic wrecks every year to equal the sacrifice demanded annually by this leering god of lust and greed in the United States alone!** It has been shown by actual figures, based upon thorough investigation, that 120,000 of the daughters of men go **every year** down into the blackness of this unspeakable traffic. That means **400 every day,** thus, **every four days,** year in and year out, equalling the number swallowed up by the sea that terrible Monday morning. Four hundred every day of the girls of America go down to death—and such a death! Drowned in the ocean! Why, that is beautiful in comparison. Rather a million times see my little ones, with cold, stark, but innocent faces, floating upon the waves of the sea, than touched by this foulness, conceived of lust and born of devilish greed!

So I might continue. I might speak of countless railroad wrecks, of the white plague parasites of poverty, of the sweatshop, of the tenements, and that hopeless, helpless, grinding want that consumes annually the best life of one-fifth of our nation. But I forbear. None of these but is alone worse than countless foundering Titanics. Those who die by these social plagues die by inches, in a sordid, soul-killing environment; and they tumble into their nameless graves—in the Potter's Field, thousands of them—with their last, awful thought, "No man cares for my soul." But the victims of the ocean liner suffered for a few moments, in an heroic environment, sustained by their mutual courage and unselfishness, knowing that their loved ones who escaped would be tenderly cared for by a waiting, sympathetic world.

III

LESSONS

Here beginneth the first lesson.

The underlying cause of it all is our social allegiance to the twin gods of Mammon, **speed** and **greed;** or, rather, let me say, to the great god Greed, and Speed, his hand maiden. Well spake the prophet, when he said, "The love of money is the root of all evil." Greed for profit built the greatest ship in the world, and equipped her for the greatest speed; greed for profit refused a sufficient number of life boats, and even refused the man in the lookout a glass that he might foresee approaching danger; greed for profit ignored repeated warnings of icebergs ahead. Why? That the Titanic might break all records. Why? That the White Star Line might get their competitors' business. Why? That the White Star Line might declare greater dividends. No more terrible indictment of our modern competitive industrial system was ever written than this.

But it's the same old, old reason that underlies all these other more terrible evils I have named. Greed furnishes defective rails, whose breaking throws express trains into the ditch. Greed refuses safety devices in mines and factories. Greed grinds out the life of the little child-slave. Greed, by refusing a living wage, throws thousands of girls onto the street to keep body and soul together. Greed leases houses for immoral purposes, maintains the "pimp" and the "cadet," exploits tenements unfit for human habitation, conducts sweatshops, feeds tuberculosis and submerges one-fifth of the nation in a hopeless state of poverty. **Greed puts profit above human rights or human welfare, and makes human life and human character the cheapest things on the market.** And all this terrible, sickening, incessant sacrifice of man's most price-less gifts goes to feed the never-satisfied maw of the grinning, leering God of Seven Per Cent!

Brethren, it's time to apply the emergency brake!

GOD'S LAW IMMUTABLE

We learn again from this disaster the lesson that **God's laws are immutable.** We thought we knew that before, but our conduct wit-nesses otherwise. In the ages of myth and fable the hand of God would have been represented as reaching out and saving the Titanic's men from a watery grave. But not so today. Humanity must pay the full price of its foolhardiness and vanity, the innocent with the guilty. That has been the law from the beginning, and will be forever. That mighty dic-tum that we teach, **the certainty of just retribution for sin,** stands out above the horizon of this horror like the iceberg that struck down the proud mistress of the seas. All human attempts to escape the working of that law are unavailing. Some have said, "But if God were a God of love, He would have interposed to save those who suffered for no fault of their own." Believe it not, my people. For God to do that would mean a universe of chaos. To miraculously save men from the conse-quences of sin would be to put a premium on sin. To have saved the Ti-tanic by miracle, when the blind arrogance and greed of her owners had hurled her into the arms of a forewarned death, would mean the total submergence of human responsibility, and leave man at the mercy of a changing, fitful, capricious deity. That is not God's way. He has or-dained certain great, immutable laws; He has created man so that he can learn, understand and abide by those laws; and if man does not obey, the penalty is death. Above the chaos of our man-marred world those laws stand unchanged and immutable, as the stars of heaven shone down that terrible night upon the chaos of the sea wrought by man's infatuated selfishness. It must be thus forever: and in no other way could God justify His love toward us. It will be thus till God's laws are universally obeyed; and the sooner those who prey upon their fellows realize this, the sooner will be ushered in the Kingdom of God.

HUMAN NATURE SUBLIME

And what a splendid demonstration we have had in this horror of the **innate nobility of mankind.** The pessimists who preach the doctrine of human degeneracy have had to lay their hands upon their mouths. Let him who bemoans the passing of the ages of chivalry take courage; for chivalry in its palmiest days offered nothing like this. Men died like men. The one conspicuous apparent exception was not an exception after all. **The cowardice of J. Bruce Ismay was due to the fact that the crisis did not find him in the way of duty. He was in the pursuit of gain. In his hands was the actual control of the ship. He might have saved the craft and its precious freight had he heeded the warning. But J. Bruce Ismay was there to see that the Titanic broke all records on her maiden trip, and upon his head rests the burden of responsibility. Is it any wonder he became panicky and jumped into a life-boat, while women and children drowned? Thus conscience doth make cowards of us all!**

But the men in the line of duty, the captain, whose pay for bringing the leviathan across would be less than $10 a day, the wireless operator, whose compensation is $20 a month, the officers and the crew—men who could hold up clean hands in the sight of God—these men were heroes, and feared not to die. The passengers, who had paid for safety as well as transportation, did not forget their manhood. Millionaire and peasant, soldier and civilian—there was scarce an exception. Men have said—and with the sanction of religion, God forgive them!—that human nature must be changed before the strong will cease to prey upon and trample over the weak. They have said that the only incentive to great deeds is the hope of personal gain. What a lie it is! This greatest of all sea horrors proves it a lie. **The man with a hundred million dollars stood aside and made room for his wife's serving maid. The man who has swayed continents with his pen gave place to a woman from the steerage. The railroad magnate remained on the sinking ship that a babe in arms might have his place in the lifeboat.** Hope of personal gain, indeed! Here we have again the demonstration that no really great deed was ever performed from such sordid motives. It is splendid, splendid! Though terrible the price, the verdict of history will be that it has been worth all it cost.

RELIGION NOT DEAD

Then, to me, one of the most heartening lessons is that **religion is not such a back number,** after all. I am discouraged in my soul often times at the small response to the spiritual appeal. Empty pews and dying churches are calculated to drive a sensitive preacher to madness. But a long, full look into men's hearts, such as this disaster affords, re-assures me. There is a mighty significance in the fact that Jews and Christians, Protestants and Catholics knelt in a common group about a priest and repeated the rosary. It may not have been according to the custom of all, but it was the only available expression of the religious instinct. And men always act by instinct in moments of great crisis. The program of music played by the brave orchestra as the ship went down is very symbolical of our modern life. At first they played light operas, ragtime and the popular songs of the day, typical of the thoughtless, careless, selfish, lightheartedness that fills our lives from day to day. **But, in the face of the stern reality, standing in the presence of the great mystery that lies beyond the impenetrable curtain we call death, the music became a prayer, and on bended knees the orchestra played "Nearer, My God, to Thee!"**

And men are all like that when they face a crisis sufficiently great to compel a consideration of eternal issues. **Religion is not dead, even though the people are asleep.** The function of the church is not gone, and will never be gone until the lessons of fundamental morality, so-cial justice and reverence of man for man, are learned. For on these, and these alone, hangs all harmony of man with God.

V

CONCLUSION

Now, in conclusion, let us observe this new evidence of the un-shakeable **power of an ideal.** In their last moments the victims of the wreck were true to the ideals of the years that had gone. And by ideals I mean **the moral standards of conduct that we all worship in secret.**

Those standards control action in critical hours, always and invariably. The strong died to save the weak because in their secret hearts they had always worshipped that ideal, however far they may have fallen short of it in practical life. And so great is the power of that ideal that the time is not far away when men will **live**, as well as die, in its spirit. We haven't come to this yet, socially at least, but we are approaching it. It is a heartsickening fact that dozens of those men who stepped heroically aside to make way for women and children in the boats had piled up immense fortunes by exploiting the necessities of women and children on land. Many men who would rather die than jostle a woman or a child in a life-boat had been drawing annual dividends from the proceeds of child-labor, and had fattened on the profits of those whose business it is to debauch womanhood. That is the horrible tragedy of it.

But the ideal is growing. And some day—a not too far distant day—the "unwritten law of the sea" will prevail also on the land. "The women, children and helpless first," will be the social watchword here as well as on the wave, the brotherhood of man will prevail, and the Kingdom of Heaven will be at hand. The ideal that governs men in their great moments will control them habitually. The dispatches tell us that Benjamin Guggenheim* sent this message to his wife by a powerful swimmer just before the ship went down: **"Tell her,"** he said, **"that this is a man's game, and I played it to the end. Tell her that no woman was left on board the ship because Ben Guggenheim was a coward."** Wasn't that splendid! And I foresee the approaching day when that will be the motto of all our human activities. I see the time coming when human welfare shall submerge the greed for profit and gain, and humanity shall say as one man: "This is a man's game. We'll play it like men, **all the time,** and we'll play it to the end." What a wonderful picture of the human heart in free action!

Hunger for God

And that other ideal that flashed up in the last hour, that clutched with such a grip upon our hearts, was man's hunger for harmony with

---

*First-cabin passenger Benjamin Guggenheim ran his family's mining empire.

God. They had worshipped that ideal in secret, or it would not have controlled them at the last. Always there, but denied, overshadowed, pushed aside by selfish, temporal interests, that hunger for harmony with God lives in the heart of every human creature. We try to laugh it away sometimes. With a great braggadocio we avow our freedom from such "superstitions." But it will not be still. Doubtless many of those "emancipated" passengers on the Titanic smiled with ill-concealed scorn at the peasant girl telling her beads, or scoffed in open anger at the prophet crying out for social righteousness. But in the last grim moments they were there with all the rest, peasant and million-aire, on their knees, with hands upraised and agonized face uplifted, singing "Nearer, My God, to Thee."

My people, **man in his heart of hearts is godlike!** Let us confess it, and live evermore in the strength of that confession. **All the centuries of man's inhumanity to man has not effaced the image of God in his soul.** Rather, through the years, that glorious likeness has constantly risen triumphant over the beast, a pledge of the coming time when every created soul shall stand upright, beautiful and true in the splendid image of its Maker.

Not long before his death the late Ernest Crosby,* whom to know was to love, wrote this fine poem. The sermon is all in it. There is no finer thought with which to close:

So he died for his faith. That is fine;
    More than most of us do.
But, say, can you add to that line
    That he lived for it, too?

In his death he bore witness at last
    As a martyr to truth.
Did his life do the same in the past,
    From the days of his youth?

*Ernest Crosby (1856–1907) was an anti-militarist, anti-imperialist poet, novelist, and essayist.

It is easy to die. Men have died
   For a wish or a whim,
For bravado, or passion, or pride,
   Was it harder for him?

But to live—every day to live out
   All the truth that he dreampt,
While his friends met his conduct with doubt,
   And the world with contempt—

Was it thus that he plodded ahead,
   Never turning aside?
Then, we'll talk of the life that he lived;
   Never mind how he died.

From a Sermon, St. Stephen's Church, Washington, D.C.

JAMES, CARDINAL GIBBONS (1834–1921)
Archbishop of Baltimore
April 21, 1912

The remote cause of this unspeakable disaster is the excessive pursuit of luxury. Valuable space was sacrificed in order that men and women might not lose for a day the pleasures and comforts that even on land are attainable by the few. A remarkable high speed was kept up amid grave perils for the purpose of gain, and for the same reason many hundreds of precious lives were consigned to an untimely grave. "Man liveth not by bread alone," and the American people ought to take earnestly to heart this grave warning and abate in no small measure the undue passion for material welfare and mere earthly enjoyments.

While I admire the shining examples of heroism that make this shipwreck forever memorable in human annals, I admire still more the numerous evidences of religious confidence, resignation, and prayer that we meet in the narratives of the unhappy survivors. I feel confident that the unparalleled sorrow that now rests like a cloud on two continents will revive in many hearts a latent sense of divine power and wisdom and goodness of God's rights in His own world, and of our human obligations to so conduct the social order that the existence and honor of God shall be respected. This is the cornerstone of all justice, and the neglect of it is the chief reason of our modern social and economic unrest.

"Two Civilizations," The Lutheran Herald

Decorah, Iowa
April 25, 1912

There is a strange contrast between the heroism of the men who "stood aside" that women and children might be saved, when the "Titanic" had received its mortal wound, and the deportment of the crew of the French liner "Bourgogne," when that boat was sunk in a collision with the British sailing ship "Cromartyshire" off Sable Island, July 4, 1898. There was perfect discipline on the "Titanic," and concerted action on the part of officers, passengers, and crew, to the end that the women and children should first be saved. The crowning glory of our civilization does not consist in the perfection of mechanical arts, or in the general diffusion of knowledge, or indeed in any attainment of intellect, but in this action of the men on board the "Titanic." Archibald Butt* parting with a "Kindly remember me to all the folks back home," after placing a woman passenger on a life boat, and then returning to the doomed vessel, that some other woman and child might be saved; Captain Smith swimming to where a child was drowning, grasping it and

---

*First-cabin passenger Major Archibald W. Butt was President William Howard Taft's military aide.

carrying it in his arms to a life-boat, and then swimming back to his ship to die; and when the last hope was gone, the band lining up on deck, and standing up to their knees in water as they played "Nearer, My God, to Thee," as 1,500 souls passed from life—what other civilization has held a counterpart to such heroism, such calm fulfilment of duty in the face of certain death? Our age has no greater glory than this.

It was otherwise on the "Bourgogne."

Of the 714 persons on board, 164 survived. Of these 105 were officers and members of the crew. Only one woman reached safety. The testimony of the surviving passengers told of cruelty and a total lack of discipline. Tales of inhuman murder were many. It was reported that the safety of the passengers was entirely neglected by the crew and that the officers made little effort to save lives. Members of the crew murdered passengers who attempted to get placed into the few boats that were lowered over the side.

Auguste Pourgi, one of the passengers, was in the water half an hour. He attempted to get into a boat, but was seized when he had managed to get halfway in and was thrown back into the water. He tried again and was again thrown out, but managed at last to get in and stay in. Clinging to the life line of a boat not far away he saw his mother, and he was forced to watch a man shove her into the ocean with an oar. She never rose. The man was saved.

Charles Lebra, who lost his two children, said that he saw five women who were evidently exhausted, clinging to the life-line of a boat. The French sailors cut the lines and the women sank.

Gustave Crimaux, a French passenger, corroborated the other passengers in their statements about the crew. They did not attempt to get any boats loose, he said, except those they needed for themselves. He saw women shoved away from boats with oars, and not only shoved away, but pushed deep into the water.

A strange contrast to the deportment of the "Titanic's" crew, is it not? Evidently Anglo Saxon civilization, under the influence of Protestant Christianity, has developed a different fibre from that of Latin civilization. The veneer of culture counts for little when women struggling in shipwreck are pushed under water with an oar. It were not reasonable to attribute such action merely to "panic." The fault lies deeper.

Those men of the "Bourgogne" who cut life-lines to which women were clinging, were products of another civilization than that which produced the heroes of the "Titanic." They were products of a civilization that knows no Bible.

From *The Titanic Tragedy—God Speaking to the Nations*

ALMA WHITE (1862–1946)
Founder of the Pillar of Fire Church, Minister, Feminist
Zarephath, New Jersey
1912

When a person has only one chance for life, there can be no worse crime than to keep the truth from him. To let hundreds of people thus die without giving them proper warning is worse than heathen barbarity. It was simply opening a trap door to let them sink down into the deep without an opportunity to try to make their escape or to call upon God the master of ocean and earth and sky.

Men unaccustomed to uttering the name of Christ, except in profanity, will often pray when facing death. The dying thief prayed and found mercy. And who knows but what a prayer meeting on board the ship would have averted the calamity and startled the world.

A murderer in his cell is not refused the privilege of having a spiritual adviser, but there was no one to whom the 1,635 souls on the doomed vessel could speak in their last moments.

We remember of hearing when a child of ships being so seriously disabled at sea that the officers lost nearly all hope, and in every instance the passengers were warned, and when prayer was unceasingly made, help came from some source. But not so on this occasion. The last remark the captain made was, "Every one for himself." But it was too late.

If some of the spiritual sons of John Wesley of a hundred years ago had been in authority on the Titanic, there would have been quite a different scene. If men had repented and called upon the Almighty, He would have heard and answered prayer.

But everything was suppressed, no one was allowed to know the truth until the waves were about to sweep them off the decks. God's curse is upon secrecy. The Scripture says there is nothing hid that shall not be revealed, and that which is spoken in the ear in the closet shall be proclaimed upon the housetops. Britons pride themselves on their ability to conceal facts, and much could be said in favor of their seamanship, but to keep secret that which concerns hundreds of human lives is criminal. There had been so much said about the unsinkable ship, people seemed to forget that God could sink anything that man could construct. One of the designers of the Titanic on board suppressed fear by declaring that the ship could not sink, that he had built it himself.

"Weekly Reflections," Bicz Bozy (God's Whip)

"CARABUS"
April 28, 1912
Translated from the Polish by Ursula Klingenberg

The Titanic went under—a thousand and seven hundred
Lost their lives in the depths of the ocean.
To think of this misfortune without grief is impossible,
Many a person will secretly shed a tear over it . . .
The disaster seems to have moved the whole earth,
And everybody is asking: what was it all for?

What was it for?—Well, the answer is easy,
It's not difficult to grasp who bears the guilt,
Even though the mercenary press muddles up matters,
Trying to conceal the causes of the accident,
And stirs up one new lie after another,
Feeding tales and humbug to childish people.

Meanwhile the naked truth shows through the lie:
The ship sank conquered by forces of nature,
(That it was the "safest" was a common ruse),
But the passengers who went down with it,
Of their terrible deaths, the loss of many lives—
Guilty are the capitalists, owners of the ship.

Indeed! Just think: for economy, for greater profit,
There were not enough boats on the ship;
If there had been—the accident wouldn't have occurred,
But a lifeboat is unnecessary, it weighs too much:
Better take some goods instead, after all . . .
Safety? Claptrap! The world has plenty of people . . .

Anybody who stops to think will grant my argument.
There is no baloney in what I say, is there?
To persuade people that there are different causes for the accident—
Would be a tendentious lie without any substance:
After a thorough examination of the accident,
Nobody can honestly say anything different.

Can't they? But look my friends, there are some here
Who explain the accident in much different terms:
Thus idlers clad in cassocks and cowls can say
That the death of one thousand and seven hundred
Must not be blamed on the ship's bosses:
It only clearly manifests "the hand of God."

They see in it punishment for sinners' transgressions . . .
They see in it punishment for human pride . . .
Punishment for man's ascent to the heights
Man who wants to become a Titan—man, a wretched creature!
And they roar to bring out the fear in everybody with their screams:
—Remember, miserable wretches, your knowledge is for nothing!—

Such an advocate does capitalism find in the ecclesiastic,
The priest justifies all crimes with divine providence . . .
Always trying to obscure the clear light of truth

With his tender and keen Augur's eye.
And when he bars all access to the truth,
He may also find something for this humbug in the collection plate.

From a Sermon, St. Bartholomew's Church, New York

REVEREND LEIGHTON PARKS (1852–1938)
April 21, 1912

Above all of the sorrow of the time, above the cries of the suffering, the hysterical shrieks of those who are well-nigh insane with their grief, there comes one strong, clear word, "Be with us and comfort all," the message of the noble-minded widow of the gallant commander of the *Titanic* to a sorrowing world. Let us leave to the Government the investigation of the great disaster, to the newspapers the repetition of its horrors, and to public opinion to award the crown of honor or the infamy of cowardice. And let us inquire if those men, who were not afraid to die, have died in vain.

You and I will be better in life and in death because of their good example. The real message of this great and overwhelming affliction is that it is the latest revelation of the power of the cross. Not all those who cry "Lord, Lord," are followers of Christ, he taught us, but they who do the will of the Father, and he also said that those who are not against him are for him.

Some of those people, who could only look back on a foolish, wasted past, acquitted themselves like men. The Master taught us to be strong and to do what we do in love. Those men were strong, and did what they did in love. We have plenty of examples of bravery—at Marathon, in the charge at Gettysburg, in the assault at Cold Harbor. But those men were soldiers, with leaders in whom they had confidence, with training and the power of discipline.

The men who stood on that deck, in the presence of disaster, exhibited a power of self-restraint, exhibited it so quietly, too, that it can not be explained on any ground of mere evolution.

Certainly, it was not a case of the survival of the fittest. There were men lost that the city and the country needed, and there are widows surviving who speak no language that you or I can understand, and who will inevitably become public charges.

They did not ask why, nor if any helpless, poor creature were worth saving. The maxims of commerce were forgotten. There was no question of buying cheap and selling dear. They sold themselves for naught; they gave their lives away. Such a sacrifice can not be justified on any economic ground.

But the Son of Man came into a world that was lost. And so the men on the *Titanic* sacrificed themselves for the women and children. The women did not ask for the sacrifice, but it was made. Those women who go about shrieking for their "rights" want something very different.

From a Sermon, Temple Beth-El, New York

RABBI SAMUEL SCHULMAN
April 20, 1912

I knew Isidor Straus for fourteen years. He was a man with a great intellect, a sensitive conscience, a great heart, a loyal son of his people, and a loyal American—a great man.

God's ways are not our ways. Therefore we should not attempt to define His motive in this tragic end of a great person. God sometimes, in His infinite wisdom, selects a man to designate that his life may be remembered by all mankind. At the conclusion of the Civil War it seemed to every one that the life of Abraham Lincoln was complete. His work, a great work, had been accomplished. Yet God saw one thing lacking. To perpetuate through the annals of time itself, one thing was essential. And God designated him and made a martyr of him.

Isidor Straus was a great Jew. All the traditions of the Jew were dear to his heart. In the past we, as Jews, have been able to say the Jews are great philanthropists. Now when we are asked, "Can a Jew die bravely?"

there is an answer in the annals of time. When we are asked, "What enabled Isidor Straus to do all these things?" our answer must be, "God blessed him and gave him Ida Straus." Isidor and Ida Straus were two persons with a single thought. Beloved and adored of each other in life, in death they were not separated.

From a Sermon, The Independent Religious Society, Chicago

MANGASAR MUGURDITCH MANGASARIAN (1859–1943)
Founder of the Independent Religious Society, College Professor
April 21, 1912

"Noblesse Oblige"—that glorious human precept was strictly observed by the splendid crew and passengers of the stricken *Titanic*. "Be Britishers!" cried the veteran Captain Smith through a megaphone from his bridge. There is nothing more inspiring in any of the Bibles in the world, except it be the more universal and thrilling challenge, "Be men!" The *Titanic* episode has vindicated human nature grandly. Jew and Christian and agnostic forgot race and religion to remember that they were men.

"The Triumph of Man," The Christian Century

May 2, 1912

Since the Titanic went down the voice of the cynic has been conspicuously silent. The cynic likes to cast slurs at manhood, to impute ignoble motives to noble deeds and to discount every story of apparent unselfishness with a sneer.

But the sublime chivalry of those who went down with the fated ship has revealed manhood's essential glory so plainly that no man dares to occupy the seat of the scorner. It is estimated that the material loss of the great vessel and her cargo was about fifteen millions of dollars. But over against that loss is to be placed the incalculable increment by which our common humanity has been enriched. The bravery, the self-control, the chivalry, the self-sacrifice, of passengers and crew have passed into the life of mankind, so that the value of every man has been enhanced thereby.

At first report the details of this event framed themselves in a ghastly picture with nature's forces in the foreground crushing man and defeating his purposes. In conflict with the vast powers of material nature, represented by the sea and the iceberg and the night, man seemed puny. How small, how helpless he is in the midst of the material order! As if to break his proud boasting, nature broke in two his "absolutely unsinkable ship" as Sampson broke the withes that bound him.

But this first impression of the meaning of the tragic picture changes as the picture is studied. Gradually nature with her forces recedes into the background, leaving man to occupy the central place. The big thing in the picture, the significant thing, the vast *motif* in the design of the mighty Artist, is not nature, not physical force, not fate, not defeat, not death, but manhood and manhood triumphant over all material forces.

Let us not name the picture "The Failure of Man," simply because his boat went down with the waves and Death swept sixteen hundred souls off the deck like the player sweeps the chess-men off the board when the game is done. But let us name the picture, "The Triumph of Man," for in his death and his failure Man was never so glorious and Death never so helpless.

The disaster sets out in bold relief the fact that man actually has triumphed over the sea. The sinking of the Titanic was not the rule but the exception to the rule. It is not the rule for man's boats to sink. It is the rule for them to make their port. The wonderful thing about sea travel is not that the Titanic went down but that ten thousand vessels reach port. It is years since the life of a passenger has been lost at sea.

The picture shows no good reason for discounting man's power to control nature for his own designs.

But it is the moral greatness of man that stands revealed in the picture in outlines of increasing clearness as the days pass into weeks and we get a truer perspective in which to view the disaster. That there was no panic, no wild scramble each man for himself, shows how far our humanity has ascended from the customs of the jungle. No wonder the cynic is dumb as he views this aspect of the picture. It is his theory that a man will give anything for his life, that apparent unselfishness is always alloyed with mean self-regard, that when a man is driven to his extremity he will act on motives of self-interest. Small comfort for the cynic in this picture of the Titanic! "Women and children first!" is the command to which the brave souls of crew and passengers yielded active and willing obedience.

And these were not the pick of humanity who stood in such admirable discipline while the women and children filled the life boats. They were not carefully selected moral leaders, whose souls had been trained and tested by special disciplines. They were the "common run" of our humanity—first class, second class and third class passengers, yes, and first class, second class and third class men. There were first class men among the third class passengers and third class men among the first class passengers. The sixteen hundred who went down were typical of mankind. And in their courage and discipline and self-control they glorified the race of humanity which they represented. They revealed not merely what man is at his highest but what he is at the average.

Yes, manhood triumphed when the Titanic sank.

But not until we take a point of view before the picture from which we can see Man facing Death do we grasp the deepest *motif* of the Artist. Death stands in the picture with a leer of triumph on his face. But it is a fading leer, a fading triumph. The exultation with which he came upon the scene to work his work of desolation is still depicted on his face, but something else is depicted on his face. He seems to see the failure of his own success; he sees that he is defeated in the moment of his triumph.

And then we look at Man. Shuddering, yes, as the cold sea creeps up around him. But he stands with his cap in his hand gallantly waving at his dear ones in the life boat! This is not Death's victory; this is Man's victory. This is not Man's death; it is Death's death.

With the brave musicians playing until their instruments filled with water, with a millionaire stepping out of a life boat in which his wife was being saved to make room for a woman, with a soldier seizing and firmly pulling back a single panic stricken man who had broken the discipline and was leaping into a boat, with a young woman giving up her place to a mother whose children needed her to live, and, after all had gone down, with the captain and his first mate each seizing a little child and leaping from the bridge into the cold sea—with details like these filling up the composite of the picture, think you, O cynic, that you can ever open your mouth again in detraction of the Man whom God made?

Editorial, The Mennonite

Berne, Indiana
April 25, 1912

When such appalling disaster occurs, when the sad news flashed through the land and the sad particulars become known, it takes a little while even for the Christian to find the right point of view. How could God, the merciful, permit such a catastrophe to occur?

It is true, that in one sense God did not do it. The disaster of the beautiful ship, provided with all modern safety appliances, happened according to the unalterable laws of God in nature. There are rumors afloat, that even human vanity, recklessness and greed caused the wreck. Can we blame God for men's faults? Yet the prophet Amos said: 3:6: "Shall there be evil in a city and the Lord has not done it?" If not one sparrow shall fall on the ground without our Father and the very hairs of our head are all numbered, how could our dear sister Funk, sped on the way by the love for a dear sick parent, perish thus?*

This is one side, the sorrow caused by the death of so many dear ones. But is there not another side to the question? Have not many men become so proud, that they think there is no God and have no use for God? And when the passengers of the doomed vessel were waiting for the last moment and the fatal plunge, how many would have dared to confess in the face of death: "there is no God"?

The band is said to have played hymns while the hundreds of passengers waited for death to come slowly, but inevitably. It is said, that with "Nearer, my God, to thee" played and sung the vessel sank.

The spirit of God had time and the opportunity to work on and prepare many to meet their Maker, who perhaps would have gone on in the mad race for gain, pleasure or fame.

But were not dear children of God on the ship? Yes there were, and they are mourned and missed by their loved ones. We miss them, we sadly feel their loss, but we need not mourn for them, for they have gone to their reward, they are with the Savior, whom they loved, and there in eternal bliss they are waiting for us.

"The Unspeakable Disaster,"
The Baptist Courier

Greenville, South Carolina
April 25, 1912

The world has been appalled by the disaster which befell the Titanic off the coast of New Foundland on Sunday night, April 14. No other sea calamity of modern times has made such an impression on the imaginations of men or has spread such universal awe. The ship belonged to

---

*Second-cabin passenger Annie Funk, a Mennonite missionary in India, was returning to the United States to visit her sick mother.

the White Star Line and was on its first voyage. It was the largest vessel ever made, and because of its water-tight compartments, was
thought to be unsinkable. An experienced seaman said "it was the last
word in sea building." Men never felt more secure on water than those
who took passage on the Titanic at Southampton, England. But the
strength, skill and device of man were never more futile. The shock with
the iceberg came at 11:40 at night and at 2:20 the great ship went
down. Of its more than 2,300 passengers only 745 were saved. One es-
timate places the number of those who perished at 1,635. There were
several men on board whose names are household words in many lands,
and all of these were lost. Not a single passenger of international note
escaped.

It is yet too early to fix responsibility, if there is any to be fixed.
Many of the criticisms which were made, when the news of the disaster first reached us, have been shown to be without foundation. The
ship did not take the northern route as was said. It took the southern.
It was not heedless of the warnings concerning icebergs, but on receiving these warnings came sixty miles still further south. It was not
trying to break the world's record but was making the ordinary speed
of fast-sailing vessels. At least these are the things now said. We should
hold all condemnatory judgment in reserve until the official investigation is made public. There was one defect which every one recognizes,
the utterly inadequate number of life-boats on the ship. The cause for
this is to be looked for in the laws of England and also in the overconfidence of the safety of the ship.

It was an unspeakable disaster. But there was that for which we can
all thank God. It was the occasion for the display of some of the di-
vinest virtues the world has ever seen. Men and women, like true Christians, sacrificed life itself to save others; and this great sacrifice was
made not merely for members of their own families. Col. Astor* after
placing his wife in the life boat spent the remaining time allotted him
in calming the fears of poor women and in helping them to places of
safety. And what was true of him was also true of many others. When
we think of the going down of that ship into those icy waters and hear

*First-cabin passenger John Jacob Astor, the wealthiest victim of the disaster.

the dying cries of hundreds of our fellow mortals in their vain struggle for life we shudder and weep; but after all, the world is richer today because of the Titanic disaster, richer in the sympathy that binds classes together, richer in heroism and self-sacrifice.

To us the disaster is a judgment of God, not a judgment on those who suffered and perished. They were but the sacrifice that was offered for the world. It takes some such calamity as that to shake men into the realization that human life is most precious of all possessions; and that no care or no cost is too great that seeks to protect it. All ships will now have life boats; and perhaps a thousand danger places on land and sea will be better guarded.

We believe also that the faith of men in the God of the Bible will be somewhat revived by this awful event. As no other happening of modern times it recalls those great events which in the Bible are called "judgments of God." It set man's confidence at naught. It came at midnight. When it came men were eating, chatting, sleeping, playing cards. Even when the great ship had been torn apart and was sinking not a man dreamed that anything much had happened. The game of cards was renewed, and young fellows picked up pieces of the ice that were thrown over the deck, and proposed to keep them as mementoes of the occasion. And thus it was. The minute touches of great Scripture passages seems to have been reproduced. Surely all men will read with a renewed faith Christ's eternal warning "Be ye also ready."

"Save Our Souls," The Herald and Presbyter

Cincinnati, Ohio
April 17, 1912

The whole world has been shocked and appalled by the great disaster of the sinking of the steamship Titanic, in which fifteen hundred persons lost their lives. The marvel is that, far away from sight of land or of any other vessel, the 705 should have escaped. They would not, and could not, have been rescued had it not been for the recently-invented wireless telegraph, by means of which the cry for help was sent out in all directions for hundreds of miles, and which brought to the relief of those who had been sent out on rafts and in lifeboats the steamer which carried them to land.

Out from the wireless instrument on the Titanic clicked out the letters, "S. O. S," in three dots, two dashes, and three dots, over and over again repeated, until they were caught and help came flying to the point of latitude and longitude given to definitely describe the location of the sinking vessel. The former signal of "C. Q. D," explained as "Come Quickly; Danger," has given place to the more readily-discerned "S. O. S," which signal is interpreted as "Save Our Souls." There was no hesitation in flinging this cry out into the universe, in the hope that the attention of some steamer might be arrested and rescue might be made possible. Nor was there any hesitancy on the part of the rescuers, when that cry for help reached them, in piling on the coal, deviating from their course, and hastening to the rescue of life. Nor has there been any one to sneer cynically, nor to criticize harshly, the excited outcry for help nor the swift response to the pleading utterance. When the cry, "Save Our Souls," came from the Titanic, the whole world prayerfully applauded the Carpathia for its prompt and effective response.

But there are multitudes in the world all around us who are in terrible danger and who should be crying to God with earnest pleading for the salvation of their souls. On the very brink of the eternal world, unprepared and unconcerned, millions are standing to-day. They ought to be praying with all their hearts to God for his salvation. Fifteen hundred lives were lost when the Titanic went down. Since then many, many times as many persons have passed from earthly life into eternity. We are startled when the ship goes down, but fifty times the number who went to death from that steamer are called on to die every day of every year. Why should we not be startled every day? Why should we not hear and heed the cry, "Save Our Souls," that is going up, or should be going up, every day, from scores of thousands who are just about to die.

There are those who antagonize any expressions of religious interest on the part of those who may be spiritually awakened, and who would hush into silence any manifestations of zeal on the part of those who would help direct their friends and fellows to salvation in Jesus Christ. This indifference to spiritual and eternal things is appalling! In view of all the perils that surround immortal souls, and of all the eternal interests that are at stake, there should be the most earnest crying out to God from all the unsaved millions for salvation and the most earnest missionary and evangelistic enthusiasm and fervor on the part of the whole Christian world in leading the multitudes to God.

"The Last Call!" The Baptist Record

Jackson, Mississippi
April 25, 1912

We are on the last week of the collections for Home and Foreign Missions. Next Sunday's work will tell the story of success or failure so far as our collections are concerned. The wireless call for help has come from hundreds of millions of men and women going down in the night from the sinking craft of false religion and no religion to the bottomless abyss of despair! The Great Captain is on the bridge of the good ship "Rescue" looking for the souls lost in the night of sin. The engineers are making speed with all their might to reach them before it is too late. All of us must help to feed the fires that hasten the ship on its way to the lost. Let them not rise up in the judgment against us. The fuel for these fires are our contributions to the work. We can afford to let everything go in; we cannot afford to withhold anything that would save a soul from hell. The next year's work will be laid out by the results of this year, and so we are making it possible or impossible for the work to be enlarged. And as we furnish the fuel of our contributions, let us turn into the furnace the blast of earnest prayer to fan the flames of effort to white heat. Lord, hear our cry, and may we hear His call.

Mistaken Emotion, The Lutheran Standard

Columbus, Ohio
May 4, 1912

Were we given our free choice, we would have nothing to say editori-ally about the shipwreck of the Titanic. There is so much hysteria evi-dent in what is being said by hundreds and thousands of speakers and writers on the subject, that one dislikes to join the ranks of the mor-alizers. But we feel that our readers would charge us with neglect if we were to allow so notable an event to pass by without mention; for which reason we will indulge in a few reflections in connection with the steamer's loss.

Why does the world act as though something so unusually sad had taken place when this terrible catastrophe occurred, while the same world allows happenings of far greater gravity to pass entirely unno-ticed?

About fifteen hundred people reached the end of their temporal life when the great sea-monster went to her watery grave. Considering that thousands and thousands of people die every day, why do we stand aghast at the thought that fifteen hundred died in this calamity? Is death so unusual an event? Is death's harvest otherwise so scant? Are we accustomed to stand in such reverence of death in general?

Again. How many thousand heathen souls pass on into the eter-nal judgment of God every minute—and we have not even made an ap-proach at doing what might be done to prepare for them a happy death in Jesus Christ, their Redeemer. How can thinking Christian people go to sleep in peace on any evening when during that day thousands of heathen have died a heathen death? Is the depth of the sea a more dread place to which to go than the judgment of Almighty God?

Those who died in the Titanic's wreck had ample time, and had un-doubtedly had ample opportunity, to make their peace with God. They were probably all souls who had had opportunities to hear and to heed the call of the gospel. Why make more ado about their death than about that of many times their number whom our tardiness has kept from enjoying the comfort of the preaching of Christ's cross?

This is not an appeal for hard-heartedness, for stolidity in the face of calamity. It is well that the entire world should shed a tear when fifteen hundred of its dwellers pass into eternity on the awful crest of one destruction's wave. But, could we not do the one, and at the same time not leave the other undone? Could we not show sympathy at the hearing of this terrible tale of the sea, and at the same time have an intelligent sympathy with others of our fellow men, who are facing direr calamities—a sympathy which would provoke us to more zealous missionary activity?

From *Christianity and Liberalism*

J. GRESHAM MACHEN (1881–1937)
Theologian
1923

The Christian doctrine of the atonement, therefore, is altogether rooted in the Christian doctrine of the deity of Christ. The reality of an atonement for sin depends altogether upon the New Testament presentation of the Person of Christ. And even the hymns dealing with the Cross which we sing in Church can be placed in an ascending scale according as they are based upon a lower or a higher view of Jesus' Person. At the very bottom of the scale is that familiar hymn:

> Nearer, my God, to thee,
> Nearer to thee!
> E'en though it be a cross
> That raiseth me.

That is a perfectly good hymn. It means that our trials may be a discipline to bring us nearer to God. The thought is not opposed to Christianity; it is found in the New Testament. But many persons have the impression, because the word "cross" is found in the hymn, that there is something specifically Christian about it, and that it has something to do with the gospel. This impression is entirely false. In reality, the cross that is spoken of is not the Cross of Christ, but our own cross; the verse simply means that our own crosses or trials may be a means to bring us nearer to God. It is a perfectly good thought, but certainly it is not the gospel. One can only be sorry that the people on the *Titanic* could not find a better hymn to die by than that.

SONGS

Rei

חורבן טיטאניק אדער
דער נאסער קבר

The Titanic's Disaster.

WORDS BY
SOLOMON SMALL
(SMULEWITZ)

Piano 50 ¢

HEBREW PUBLISHING CO.
83-87 CANAL ST.   NEW YORK
COPYRIGHT   1912

ARRANGED FOR PIANO BY
H. A. RUSSOTTO

Violin 30 ¢

J. KEILER

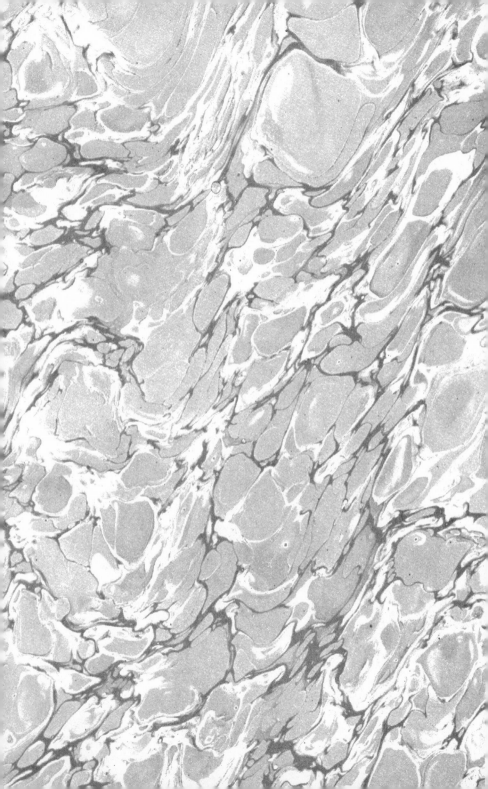

God Moves on the Water

VERSION SUNG BY LIGHTNIN' WASHINGTON
Darrington State Farm, Texas
Recorded in 1933

Chorus

God moves on the water,
God moves on the water,
God moves on the water,
And the people had to run and pray.

In the year of nineteen and twelve,
On-a April the thirteenth day,
When the great *Titanic* was sinkin' down,
Well, the peoples had to run and pray.

When the lifeboat got to the landin',
The womens turned around
Cryin', "Look 'way cross that ocean, Lawdy,
At my husband drown."

Cap'n Smith was a-lyin' down,
Was asleep for he was tired;
Well, he woke up in a great fright,
As many gunshots were fired.

Well, that Jacob Nash was a millionaire,
Lawd, he had plenty of money to spare;
When the great *Titanic* was sinkin' down,
Well, he could not pay his fare.

Down with the Old Canoe

VERSION SUNG BY THE DIXON BROTHERS
Darlington County, South Carolina
Recorded in 1938

It was twenty-five years ago
When the wings of death came low
And spread out on the ocean far and wide
A great ship sailed away
With her passengers so gay
To never never reach the other side

Chorus

Sailing out to win her fame
The Titanic was her name
When she had sailed five hundred miles from shore
Many passengers and her crew
Went down with that old canoe
They all went down to never ride no more

This great ship was built by man
That is why she could not stand
She could not sink was the cry from one and all

But an iceberg ripped her side
And He cut down all her pride
They found the Hand of God was in it all

Your Titanic sails today
On life's sea you're far away
But Jesus Christ can take you safely through
Just obey his great commands
Over there you're safe to land
You'll never go down with that old canoe

When you think that you are wise
Then you need not be surprised
That the hand of God should stop you on life's sea
If you go on in your sins
You will find out in the end
That you are just as foolish as can be

The Great Titanic

Version from Hackleburg, Alabama
Recorded in 1915

It was on one Monday morning just about one o'clock
When that great Titanic began to reel and rock;
People began to scream and cry,
Saying, "Lord, am I going to die?"

Chorus

It was sad when that great ship went down,
It was sad when that great ship went down,
Husbands and wives and little children lost their lives,
It was sad when that great ship went down.

When that ship left England it was making for the shore,
The rich had declared that they would not ride with the poor,
So they put the poor below,
They were the first to go.

While they were building they said what they would do,
We will build a ship that water can't go through;
But God with power in hand
Showed the world that it could not stand.

Those people on that ship were a long ways from home,
With friends all around they didn't know that the time had come;
Death came riding by,
Sixteen hundred had to die.

While Paul was sailing his men around,
God told him that not a man should drown;
If you trust me and obey,
I will save you all to-day.

You know it must have been awful with those people on the sea,
They say that they were singing, "Nearer My God to Thee."
While some were homeward bound,
Sixteen hundred had to drown.

The Titanic

Version from Southern Michigan
Recorded in 1931

The *Titanic* left Southampton
With all its sports and gang;
When they struck the iceberg,
I know their mind was changed.

Chorus

Many hearts surrendered to the shipwreck;
On the sea many hearts surrendered,
Crying, "Nearer, My God, to Thee."

The fourteenth day of April,
Nineteen hundred and twelve,
The ship wrecked by the iceberg
Went down forever to dwell.

The story of the shipwreck
Is most too sad to tell;
One thousand and six hundred
Went down forever to dwell.

Mothers told their daughters
On a pleasure trip they might go;
But since they struck the iceberg,
They haven't been seen any more.

A man, John Jacob Astor,
A man with pluck and brains,
When that great ship was going down,
All the women he tried to save.

Our Sea Heroes

Words by Miss E. J. Thibaut, Music by Charles J. W.
Jerreld
1912

Carried away down in the Atlantic,
Calm and brave our men stood upon the Titanic;
Amid the horror they ne'er forgot honor,

They cried save children and women,
I'm the strongest of the race,
I'm the man.

God place our heroes, of the sea;
Nearer to Thee, Nearer to Thee.

Never shall we forget their bravery,
Their sacrifice has immortalized their mem'ry;
We honor them all the humble and the high,
Like bravest soldiers they died,
For the woman and also, for the child.

Wreck of the "Titanic"

WORDS AND MUSIC BY REGINALD M. TEWKSBURY
1912

Only an iceberg,
Oh! but the woe it spread;
As o'er the ocean,
The bodies of brave lie dead;

Fathers and mothers
Torn from their lov'd ones so dear,
Drifted so mutely,
'Neath the moon so clear!

Refrain

Oh! could those dear ones be called back again,
Oh! could the story be told without pain;
Heaven be merciful to those that are gone,
Heroes, All brave, Ever thy loss we'll mourn.

Adrift in the lifeboats,
Out on the seas so drear;
Wives, Mothers, Sweethearts,
There mingled in throes of fear;

Theirs is the sorrow,
Comes to the low and the high,
In home or hovel,
Under moonlit sky!

Just Whisper the Message

WORDS AND MUSIC BY THOMAS H. MULVEY
1912

The lights were softly beaming o'er the brilliant ball-room floor,
    The music softly sheeling sweetly echoed o'er and o'er,
The fragrance of crushed violets came wafted on the air,
    The scene was one of grace and splendor fair;
As soft and low the strains awoke a waltz of beauty rare,
    A youth and maid in rapture circled by,
He gently drew her closer, pressed the little hand so fair,
    And fondly crooned the old familiar air.

Chorus

Just whisper the message a fond heart will hear,
    Just softly, sweetly breathe it "Honey Dear,"
Like a zephyr of spring, let it fall from your lips,
    To a poor aching heart, bringing cheer.

'Mid throngs of happy dancers in the liner's "Grand Saloon,"
    The youth and maid were planning for the wedding day in June,

He said, "My own sweet loved one, life for me has just begun,"
    And on each word the sweet-souled maiden hung;
Then rang a crash, and dark dismay swept o'er the maiden fair,
    The youth in vain, the wreckage braved to stay,
They wrapped him in The Colors, for the souls he died to save,
    They heard her to his mute lips strangely pray.

The night and black despair reigned o'er the proudest ocean deck,
    Astern the eoned monster hoarsely croaked the human wreck;—
Oh, "Send out Succor," prayed the winds, "We're Sinking by the
    Head;"—
    The very winds for pity calmed in dread;—
Stilled was the Key, but other pray'rs rose up to Heav'n above,
    As one, in awful fervor, brave men prayed,
But as the proud boat slowly settled, to a living grave,
    The sweet-heart maid in calmness blankly prayed.

From *The Wreck of the Titanic, or The Watery Grave*

WORDS BY SOLOMON SMALL (SMULEWITZ), MUSIC BY H. A.
RUSSOTTO
1912
Translated from the Yiddish by Mark Slobin

There stand, in woe
The thousands in need
And know that death
Will dash them down.
Then the cry, "Save yourselves
Into the boats quickly, women
No man dare

Take a place there."
But listen to one woman-soul
Who can say,
"I won't stir from the spot
I'll die here with my husband."
Let small and large Honor
The name of IDA STRAUS!

The Titanic

LEADBELLY (HUDDIE LEDBETTER) (1888–1949)
1912

It was midnight on the sea.
The band was playing "Nearer my God to Thee."
Fare thee, Titanic, fare thee well.

Titanic when it got its load
Captain he hollered, "All aboard."
Fare thee, Titanic, fare thee well.

Titanic was comin' round the curve
When it run into that great big iceberg.
Fare thee, Titanic, fare thee well.

When the Titanic was sinkin' down
They had them lifeboats around
Fare thee, Titanic, fare thee well.

They had them lifeboats around,
Savin' the women 'n children, lettin' the men go down,
Fare thee, Titanic, fare thee well.

Jack Johnson* want to get on board
Captain he said, "I ain't haulin' no coal,"
Fare thee, Titanic, fare thee well.

When he heard about that mighty shock,
You mighta seen a man doin' the Eagle Rock
Fare thee, Titanic, fare thee well.

*Jack Johnson was the world heavyweight boxing champion at the time of the disaster.

NEWS *and*

OTHER TIMELY
REFLECTIONS

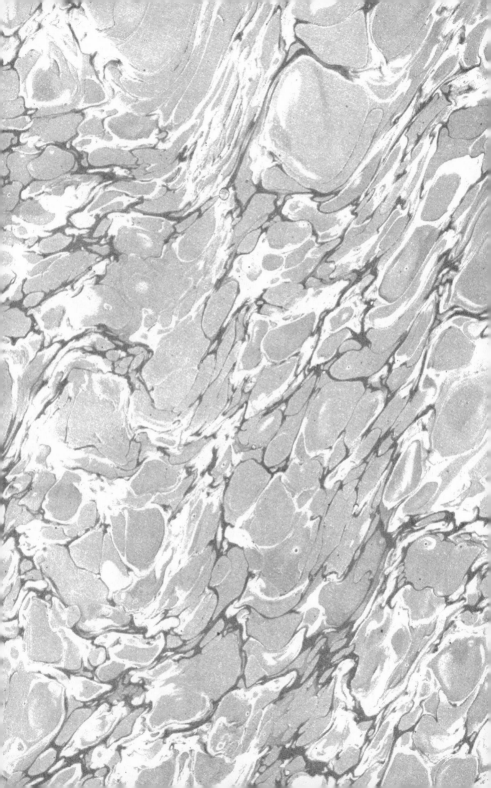

"Rich Bow to Poor,"
The San Francisco Examiner

April 17, 1912

The picture that inevitably presents itself, in view of what is known, is of men like John Jacob Astor, master of scores of millions; Benjamin Guggenheim of the famous family of bankers; Isidor Straus, a merchant prince; William T. Stead, veteran journalist; Major Archibald W. Butt, soldier; Washington Roebling, noted engineer—of any or all of these men stepping aside, bravely, gallantly remaining to die that the place he otherwise might have filled could perhaps be taken by some sabot-shod, shawl-enshrouded, illiterate and penniless peasant woman of Europe.

Thus the stream of women with toddling infants, or babes in arms, perhaps most of them soon to be widowed, filed up from the cabins and over the side and away to life.

"The Titanic Tragedy," The Appeal to Reason

Girard, Kansas
May 4, 1912

When the Titanic, the greatest ocean liner ever launched, went down to the bottom on her maiden trip, she carried sixteen hundred human beings down with her. The Titanic illustrated in herself and in her destruction within three days after she put to sea the greed and rapacity and contempt for human life which under capitalism inspired and presided over her creation.

There are a thousand reasons why this horror upon the high sea should never have occurred; why it was absolutely inexcusable and indefensible; why it was courted and inevitable, and why, in fact, it will prove in the lapse of time to have been a blessing to humanity.

Had there not been an inexperienced boy twenty years of age in charge of the wireless mechanism the passengers would all have been saved; better still, if there had been a lookout glass in the hands of the man on the bridge, which the niggardly policy of the company regarded as a useless expense, the fatal berg would have been located in time and the horrible disaster averted.

The White Star Line had millions for the wanton and wicked luxury of the pampered millionaires, but not a dollar for a lookout glass.

Had there been the requisite number of life boats aboard, not a passenger need to have been lost. These and scores of other reasons might be given for our declaring that the sixteen hundred deaths on the Titanic were *sixteen hundred deliberate, cold-blooded murders,* chargeable to the owners and managers of the White Star Line.

The Titanic was to make *a record* that was to bring a harvest of gold—*a record for profit,* for greasy lucre—and it made a record, but a different one than its owners calculated on.

The Titanic rushed headlong to her terrible fate—*in pursuit of profit.*

So much space had to be given to the private promenades, golf links, swimming pools for the plutocrats aboard that there was no space left for life-boats when the crash came. Could misdirected ingenuity, perverted taste and mental and moral insanity go farther?

Had the Titanic been a mudscow with the same number of useful workingmen on board and it had gone down while engaged in some useful social work the whole country would not have gasped with horror, nor would all the capitalist papers have given pages for weeks to reciting the terrible details.

We have been told a thousand times and with as many variations of the bravery of the rich and prominent men aboard, but very little has been heard about the bravery of *the men and women in the steerage.* We have not time for detail. But suppose we give just a moment's thought to the fifty bell boys, proletarian lads, who went down after having been shut in under command of a captain so they would not interfere with the escape of the rich first-class passengers.

The valet of Mrs. John Jacob Astor delivered to her in the life boat her costly furs and then humbly bowed himself back to the boat and *went down to the bottom.*

With two exceptions the heroes in the hold, the stokers and the men who do the work that moves every boat on every sea, and without whom not another boat would ever move an inch, went down without the ghost of a chance to escape and no one has heard of a single one of them shrinking from his tragic fate.

The steerage passengers, penned in like cattle, were long held back in the passageway with loaded revolvers pointed at them, and it was only when the rich passengers had been given all the favored opportunities to make sure of their escape that the women and children of the steerage were shown any consideration.

The one fine thing for which we give full credit to the men on the Titanic, *both rich and poor,* was that they observed the sea rule, "Women and Children First." For that we thank and honor them all without respect to station.

But would it not be a good thing to make this the rule of life instead of its extremely rare exception when a calamity enforces it?

Why not organize society on the basis of women and children first?

There are a thousand lessons to this monstrous marine disaster. We have time and space for but one or two. First, as long as profit is supreme its shocking penalties will be enforced upon men. Second, life is life, and when we come down to it the rich man's life is not worth a particle more than the life of a pauper.

John Jacob Astor went down with the stokers in the hold. In the flash of an instant they were on a level. Death equalized them, established their kinship, made them brothers. In life capitalism separated them as widely as the poles but at the supreme moment and in the presence of the infinite they were united and *stood on one common basis of equality in the democracy of death.*

Why is it that when a disaster occurs such as the sinking of the Titanic the whole world feels the shock and is thrown into hysterics, while infinitely greater tragedies are being enacted all about us in the world of industry in all of the circling hours of the day and night?

When little Leona Fugate, the poor little girl of eight, had her legs torn from her body by the murderous Metropolitan and was then robbed of her legal rights by the monstrous Judge Hook,* a darker tragedy was enacted, more human suffering was involved and a greater crime against humanity committed than when John Jacob Astor went down in the Titanic. Astor is dead and his suffering was for but an hour; little Leona lives a maimed and hopeless wreck with all the years of poverty before her to wring from her broken little heart the last despairing sigh before her blasted life is ended.

As if to enforce its supreme lessons by providential command Ismay was saved with the women and children.

Ismay, the managing director, worth one hundred million dollars and drawing an annual salary from the White Star Line of one hundred and seventy-five thousand dollars per year!

Ismay is the epitome of capitalism as revealed in the Titanic disaster. Old ocean would not receive him and he is spurned of men. And so it will soon be with the system which produced him and of which he has furnished us its most striking incarnation.

The Titanic disaster is a capitalist disaster. The evidence is overwhelming. Had the Titanic been constructed under social supervision and been socially owned and in so-

---

*Leona Fugate was run over by a streetcar operated by the Metropolitan Street Railway Company in Kansas City on January 2, 1911. On June 3, 1911, Judge William C. Hook of the U.S. Court of Appeals for the Eighth Circuit granted the Metropolitan's application for receivership, thereby preventing the collection of any personal injury claims against the company.

cial service, instead of being privately owned and launched and operated for private profit this appalling disaster would never have blackened the annals of humanity.

Just as the Titanic went down in wreck and disaster so will capitalism which she so tragically typified also go down, but it is to be hoped that when the crisis comes there may be life boats enough to carry humanity safely into the Socialist Republic.

"Men of Brains and Millions Sacrificed for Lowly Women," The Denver Post

FRANCES WAYNE
April 16, 1912

When men go down to sea in ships, chivalry flowers like the rod of Aaron.

The wreck of the Titanic serves notice to the civilized world that men are as brave and unselfish today as when poets wrote their lives and proclaimed their deeds, and by this latest ocean horror does the question rise concerning the truth or fallacy of the survival of the fittest law.

There is a law of the sea—unwritten, and unelastic—which decrees that, in times of peril, men must give way while women and children are passed to safety. It is a law which levels all social and race distinctions; a law out of which springs much injustice, if the good of society is to be balanced against individual worth. But it is a law that now and again makes creatures made in the image of God worthy of the model.

The Titanic was considered the last word in modern shipbuilding. A floating palace it was, which one must see to realize its magnificence. All that science, ingenuity and floods of money could do to make it invulnerable to the sea's hidden dangers and the sky's loosened terrors was accomplished when, from its harbor, the ship set out on its first voyage.

The steerage, new and shining, was filled with creatures weary of the dragging, dreary days of the old world—bound for what they considered liberty and the great chance. In their hands they carried all they possessed of this world's goods.

Huddling together, the chattering women envied the lovely ladies who came to look at them, wrapped warm in rich furs; the men, lifting their eyes, vowed to some day be as the elegant gentlemen who accompanied them, and the filmy-eyed children of peasants were quite willing to play with the little ones in smart sea togs, who, with their parents or nurses, were brought to look at them.

Above, we are told, were many hundreds of men and women who in their wealth, social, financial and artistic achievements topped the pinnacle of success. There were men whose services to humanity cannot be computed; there were physicians whose continued effort meant the lulling of the world's pain—the soothing of the way over which men and women are called to trudge. There was an artist who added to the beauty of life by his pictures; there were statesmen whose business it is to make nations more comfortable and friendly; there were capitalists who had never yet come upon anything they could not buy with their gold; there was a great writer, whose pen has dripped more successful reforms than judges have wrought, or parliaments made imperative. Other writers were also listed among the passengers who added to the gayety of a reading public or to the sum of human knowledge. There were beautiful women whose aim was pleasure—only.

Aboard was baggage valued at many millions of dollars; jewels that would check the arrogance of Solomon, could that potentate return and look upon them. All that adds to the value of existence cargoed that craft—and the sense of safety lay upon it. Captain Smith was one of the most experienced officers in the service and his last appointment was to guide the Titanic on its first voyage. After that he was to retire.

The great liner had made more than half the distance; the passengers from steerage to royal suite, lolled in its luxuries. The night fell clear, cold. Down the folds of the curtained darkness slid Fate, bringing Death, terror and a test whereby men were to prove themselves Men.

The Titanic plows into the solid wall of a huge iceberg that snaps its armor; sets the monster thing to shuddering as though it were a dog frightened by a ghost.

From everywhere rush men and women and whimpering children, waked from their sound sleep. There is chaos which becomes order under the captain's command. The ship founders—that it will sink is certain. Therefore, who of that vast company shall be donated to life; who to the waves!

And here steps in the law of the sea. The women and children go first—after them, if there be room, the men may have place in the lifeboats. The law is inexorable.

John Jacob Astor owns two hundred million dollars worth of property; he is newly married to a fair young woman and to them is soon to be born an heir. Chattering nearby is a peasant woman, holding fast to a low-browed man who clasps in his arms a child marked with the blight of Europe—a child that will be denied entrance to the United States after it has come before the inspectors at Ellis Island.

John Jacob Astor would give all he possesses for the place of that woman and child in the lifeboat. He is a citizen of the country toward which they are drifting; in a way, he has been among the builders, and has proved himself loyal in the time of the country's need. Why can't he now buy what he wants? Because of that law based on a sentimental ideal of manly courage and chivalry which bids men hold back, or be forever branded as cowards and bullies!

W. T. Stead,* at the very zenith of his powers, with his helpful messages to the race but half delivered, steps aside, as a scrofulous girl, limp with terror, is dragged from below and shoved into the hands of the rescuing crew. As she swings to safety, the great journalist sees the dramatic splendor and ghastly piteousness of the scene and wishes, with all the scribbler's instinct that is in him, that he could cover the story and get it onto the wires that the sleeping world beyond the horizon might know how men really do go down to sea in ships. And how he would have told that story!

There is aboard, the right arm of the president of the United States,

---

*First-cabin passenger William T. Stead was an English journalist and reformer.

Major Butt. A fine fellow and a healthy one. Hitherto this man's word has been in the nature of a command. He has been a valiant soldier, a social favorite of the first rank in the capitals where he has visited. His loudest howl for help from the deck of the Titanic—were he capable of making one—would become a murmur in the clamor of the aliens.

So Major Archibald Butt bows to the Law of the Sea and beholds a hollow-chested, blear-eyed woman, gibbering strange sounds, assigned a place in the boats while the cold waters of Death creep nearer and nearer to him and his friends. He cannot have his way, this time, any more than the millions of the millionaire can gain precedence for him. The disease-bitten child, whose life at the best is worthless, and whose value as a prospective citizen of the United States is less than worthless, goes to safety with the rest of the steerage riff-raff, while the handler of great affairs, the men who direct the destinies of hundreds of thousands of workers, the learned men whose talents are dedicated to the cure of physical afflictions; writers whose words are as burning lamps in troubled darkness, and whose energies have uplifted humanity, stand unprotestingly aside.

This acknowledgment of the Law of the Sea is the grandest exhibition that exists of the working of the code which protects the weaker element in the face of certain death, without taking note of their worthiness or fitness, and the most striking illustration of modern thought as compared with the ancient idea of "save himself who can." The Law of the Sea shows mercy without being merciful!

It leaves women helpless in their widowhood, and thrusts them on the cold charity of a society which is resentful against them for taking room that might have been given to someone who makes the world better and stronger by his presence.

Yet who can say that such leveling disasters as that which has befallen the Titanic are not good for the soul of a people grown pompous and indifferent in their conceit, and the belief that the "dollar" is the sign of power. The golden calf had come to set with adamant firmness on its pedestal of ambition and selfishness, when John Jacob Astor was made to discover that his coffers were filled with counterfeit money. The despair in the heart of the coughing peasant woman faded, perhaps, as she found that for her there was a place in the rocking boat by the side of the white-faced lady of the splendid furs.

By every law of common sense and reasoning, the passenger list of the Titanic should have been combed, and the strong men, women and children saved for the good of humanity—whether they came from below or from above deck.

The Law of the Sea is chiseled on the tablets of Time, and it cannot be changed. On its endurance depends, to a great extent, the continuance of genuine manliness, the perpetuation of pure courage, the inspiration for unselfishness; it effaces all values that are outside the man and his character, and makes for brotherhood far more than all the sermons that can be preached.

John Jacob Astor going to a sea burial is a far more important figure than John Jacob Astor ever could be by owning unusual quantities of money. Probably he stood shoulder to shoulder with a hulk of flesh from Austria or Italy and embraced "his brother" with a cheering word as the cold waters flowed over them. It is well to think so, for one in the darkness was no better than the other.

It is a piteous travesty on scientific argument—this sinking of the Titanic. It forms an illuminated page of singular beauty in the records of human courage, self-abnegation and adherence to a sentimental ideal that keeps blood warm and the heart throbbing.

Going down to sea in ships makes Julia O'Grady sit right next the colonel's lady in the lifeboat, and whatever distance exists between the shepherd's crook and the scepter is washed away.

"There Are Others," The Miners Magazine

Denver, Colorado
May 2, 1912

Since the Titanic, that great floating palace of the sea, went down to a watery grave off the grand banks of Newfoundland, the daily journals have contained many tributes to the heroism displayed on board the sinking ship, while men faced death. There is no question of doubt but that brave men stood on the deck of the Titanic and that brave men were responsible for the saving of the women and children who were passengers on the ill-fated vessel.

But the daily press that usually panders to the kings of finance, has devoted almost all of its editorial space to showering encomiums of immortal glory upon the names of the multi-millionaires who accepted the Titanic as a coffin and the ocean as a grave, rather than save their lives at the expense of women and children.

But while the daily press has immortalized the multi-millionaires as men of heroic mould, let us not forget the common men who made up the crew of the Titanic, who with pistols in their hands kept back the patrician mob, who yearned to seek safety in the life boats.

The multi-millionaires were forced to be *brave* and permit the women and children to be cared for by that courageous crew of the Titanic, whose knees did not bend in the presence of powerful magnates.

John Jacob Astor has been crowned as a *hero*, because he went down with the Titanic, while his newly made bride was saved, but the daily press did not dwell upon the fact that Astor begged to go in the life boat as the protector of his wife, but was waived back by that heroic crew whose chivalry towards women and children in the hour of peril and death, will immortalize them as the bravest of the brave.

While the daily press has eulogized the heroism of multi-millionaires who went down to watery graves on the Titanic, that press should not forget the every-day heroes of mine, railroad, mill and factory who risk life and limb, and brave death to keep in motion the industrial machinery of the world.

"Why All the Attention Directed to the Titanic Disaster?" *Editorial*, Raivaaja (Pioneer)

Fitchburg, Massachusetts
April 20, 1912
Translated from the Finnish by Timo Riippa

It is said that the Titanic was not only the largest ship in history, but also the most luxurious. The first and second class accommodations were as lavish as is humanly possible to create. But what about the life-saving equipment? There were not enough lifeboats to save everyone on board. The lifesaving equipment was reserved only for the wealthy, whose amenities were carefully attended to. For this reason, the immigrant passengers, with few exceptions, drowned.

Many things are still unclear about the Titanic disaster. But it is proper to ask whether it was necessary to attempt to set a world's speed record when the charted course passed through a part of the Atlantic where giant icebergs were known to drift.

It is also known that other ships warned the Titanic about icebergs. Despite the warnings, the Titanic sped through the dark night to achieve a world's record. It certainly set a record, but one that illustrates how thousands of lives are sacrificed when the singleminded goal is victory.

We have noticed how the American newspapers have devoted an enormous amount of space to the horror of this disaster. And it certainly was horrible.

But why do the bourgeois newspapers raise such a hue and cry about this singular event, when many equally horrible, but much costlier disasters in terms of human life, go unreported? All totaled, mining cave-ins and explosions have caused even more victims, but the bourgeois papers mention such events only in passing. Isn't a blazing mine, where human beings are burned alive, equally as horrible as a sinking ship? We think it is.

The personal worth of a typical miner in a mining disaster isn't reckoned in the hundreds of millions of dollars. It's those without property who die in the mines—the same class that drowned in large numbers with the Titanic. But certain victims have become the center of attention for the newspapers, which have published a flood of articles, computing the personal wealth of these individuals, describing how they made their money, and speculating about their life insurance policies. The bourgeois newspapers have even raised a question about carelessness with regard to human life? How moving! But when fires occur in sweatshops from time to time and loss of life climbs to hundreds and even thousands, all totaled, the capitalist newspapers keep as quiet as possible.

From "The Floating Cemetery: A Conversation Among the Drowned Ones of the Titanic," The Jewish Daily Forward

"THE PROLETARIAN"
April 28, 1912
Translated from the Yiddish by David Guralnik

How did those floating corpses die? Who knows? Some probably lived for hours, struggling against the oceanic angel of death, until they no longer had the strength to keep their mouths above water. Others probably froze to death. Still others perhaps fainted out of fright, and so were drowned. And as you imagine their helpless death struggles, you realize that all the lifebelts did was to prolong the agony.

The floating body of an aristocrat in a frock coat with gold cufflinks and delicate hands bumps into the poorly clad body of a worker with coarse, calloused hands and signs of toil in every wrinkle of the face.

"Away! Get away from me!" says the floating aristocrat with a look of revulsion on his face. "What has possessed you? Have you forgotten your place?"

A smile appears on the face of the worker. "Do you think you're still living?" answers the poorly clad one. "Where we are now, there are no privileged folks. Here we're all aristocrats."

Another poorly clad one chimes in, "Yes, here there's no privilege. Here everyone's equal. Here there's no first class, no third class. Here there are no workers who create all the good things, no non-workers who consume all the good things. Here there are no robbers who gloat over their victims. Here there is equality."

"Equality?" asks another well-clad one. "I'm wealthy, and yet they wouldn't let me into a lifeboat, while poor workers' women were given a place in the boats. Some equality."

"But we rich folks are cavaliers, gentlemen. We step aside for the women and die like heroes. The papers are full of our heroic deaths."

That brings laughter from the poorly clad. "Oy, that aristocrat fought to get into a boat but was held back by pistols. Now the papers are filled with their heroism. We poor folks who died while stoking the fires in the engine room until the very last minute, we third-class passengers who truly showed heroism, about us they write nothing. We're not interesting. We're poor folks."

"But here's one rich man," says another poor one, "who had a heart and who died like a mensch. He and his wife could have saved themselves, but they gave up their spots for others."

"So what does that prove?" says still another. "That even a millionaire can sometimes be humane and that even in this ugly world occasional rays of light pierce the darkness that would not exist if the world weren't such an ugly place?"

Some of the well-dressed ones grimaced at that.

"What's wrong, you don't like that?" asked a coal-heaver.

And so the conversation went on until it began to grow darker and a silence fell over this floating cemetery.

"The Drift of the Testimony," Editorial,
The New York Times

April 20, 1912

By the latest calculation, based on a fair comparison of the statements of the survivors, the Titanic struck the iceberg at about 11:40 o'clock (ship's time) last Sunday night, and remained afloat about two hours and forty minutes. That time might have been too short, perhaps, to muster all the people on board in orderly fashion, get them into boats, and the boats safely away from the wreck, if there had been boats enough, or nearly enough, to save everybody. The testimony of various survivors indicates that among the first-cabin passengers there was little or no alarm at first. BRIDE, the second Marconi operator, whose wonderfully graphic story of the wreck appeared in yesterday's TIMES, says that he and his brave, ill-fated principal, PHILLIPS, were in a jocular mood as the earlier calls for help were sent out. They regarded this proceeding as merely formal. The company's often-repeated assurance that the Titanic was "unsinkable" served to keep the first-class passengers calm.

Such disorderly conduct as there was, and there was enough to cause bloodshed, occurred among the steerage passengers. Some of the men were determined to save their own precious lives, in spite of the orders to let the women and children go first. Officers, with the help of some of the men passengers, tried to hold them back. The ship was so large that the noise of a scuffle in any one part of it did not reach the ears of passengers in other parts. Some of the survivors who were not eye-witnesses to any disorderly scenes, however, declare that they heard pistol shots. The heroism displayed on board in the brief interval between the hurried loading of the lifeboats and the sinking of the wreck was splendid, strengthening one's faith in humanity, attesting the willingness of men of action, with everything to live for, to die for duty's sake. But there would inevitably be men lacking courage among so many of so varied origin and training. Of the 745 passengers saved, 210 were members of the crew, an enormously unfair proportion, proving conclusively that there were cowards in the ship's company.

To offset this, there is the authentic story of one of the stewards who was asked by one of the women passengers why he did not tie a life preserver on his body. "I'm afraid there will not be enough to go round," he simply replied. There is proof of courage and devotion to duty in that answer which brings tears to the eyes. Many of the passengers testify to the courage and gentleness of the crew. The ill-behaved members did not come under their notice.

That the band was still playing as the lifeboats, or some of them, were rowed away from the ship seems to be an assured fact. BRIDE testifies that he heard the music as he jumped from the ship. The band hardly played, however, until the moment the ship sank, as she broke in the middle before that. There are the inevitable discrepancies of all collections of statements by eyewitnesses in the story touching the band and the music it played; in the uncertain record of the impressions received from the shock of the collision, which to the first-cabin passengers seemed very slight, though it must have created a panic in the steerage; and in the accounts of the lighting of the ship after the disaster. The dynamos must have given out very soon after the collision. There is testimony that the extra lights, provided by storage batteries, were then turned on. To some of the survivors in the lifeboats the Titanic seemed to be brilliantly illuminated until almost the last moment. Others saw no lights at all. This is accounted for easily by the position of the boats in relation to the wreck. Those whose occupants saw only the stern or the bow were out of the range of the lights.

When all the testimony thus far received is carefully weighed, and due allowance made for the hysterical condition of some of the survivors, the resultant impression is that there was much confusion on board, that orders were imperfectly communicated and badly carried out, that many more persons might have been saved, even with the limited number of lifeboats. If 200 more had been put in those boats, and it seems that the number of survivors might have been increased to that extent with safety, not a woman would have been drowned, and such men as ASTOR, BUTT, STEAD, STRAUS, MILLET, MOORE, and WIDENER* might have been spared to live out the term of their natural lives. But they all died nobly, and from what we have learned of the actions after the collision of men like these on the stricken vessel we are confident that not one would have cared to live an hour longer at the cost of a woman's life. They will be forever renowned as brave, generous men who died nobly.

"Sublime!" International Musician

May 1912

The sinking of the Titanic on the morning of April 15, 1912, off Cape Race, N.F., is the most awful marine disaster recorded since history was known. Much has been said as to how this dreadful tragedy

---

*Francis Millet, a painter, Clarence Moore, a sportsman and socialite, and George Widener, a street railway magnate, were first-cabin passengers.

occurred, and what was done by officers, crew and passengers after it was fully realized that the great ship had received a mortal wound in its collision with an iceberg.

Many conflicting stories have been published, and the real truth will probably never be known. It is, however, some consolation to know that the consensus of reports so far made speak well for the self sacrifice and heroism displayed by the officers, crew and passengers, regardless of official or social station.

Much as the reports differ, they are a unit in describing the sublime heroism of the ship's orchestra.

In the last supreme moment, death staring all in the face, when it was "Farewell hope, farewell fear, hail dark despair," and the ship about to plunge to her mausoleum of the sea, the ship orchestra sent forth the strains of "Nearer My God To Thee."

Hope springs eternal in the human breast. We can believe that at that supreme moment, listening to the strains of this solemn hymn, despair was changed to hope, hope for the future so near at hand. It would require a word painter such as Hugo, Beecher, or Ingersoll, to do full justice to the sublimity of this solemn moment. A reporter by the name of Hurd, who happened to be a passenger on the Carpathia, wrote a fine descriptive story as he gathered it from the survivors. Speaking of the heroism of the orchestra, he says:

"As the screams in the water multiplied, another sound was heard, strong and clear at first, then fainter in the distance. It was the melody of the hymn "Nearer My God To Thee," played by the string orchestra in the dining saloon. Some of those in the water started to sing the words, but grew silent as they realized that for the men who played, the music was a sacrament soon to be consummated by death. The serene strains of the hymn and the frantic cries of the dying blended in a symphony of sorrow."

Music is an universal language. It has no nationality, therefore the musicians of the world must take care of the dependants of these heroes. Their names will be secured, and if possible their photographs. They must be immortalized. Their names and pictures ought to hang in the place of honor wherever musicians congregate. In this country and Canada, whatever is done, should be done through the A.F. of M. to insure uniformity of action. Sporadic efforts, no matter how well meant, will not bring about near as good results as concentrated effort.

Every attempt of any one to gain personal notoriety on account of this holocaust should be promptly frowned down.

"Titanic—The Press—The Heroism of the Rich," La Fiaccola (The Torch)

"VIRTUS"
Buffalo, New York
May 4, 1912
Translated from the Italian by Bruce Venarde

The giant of the transatlantics was near the end of its maiden voyage. The shareholders of the White Star Line, who had given orders to its captain to make every effort to break all the "records," and thus be able to multiply a hundredfold their shares in the shortest time possible, waited anxiously for this mighty and enormous ship to surprise the whole world, and a moderate number of American millionaires, in the vast and gilded ballrooms of the Titanic, were rejoicing in a delightful voyage, without even the slightest idea that any natural element could sink all at once so grandiose a piece of work.

But through a lack of foresight resulting from the thirst for publicity, which in a short time had swollen the wallets of White Star shareholders, all illusions were reduced to nothing, to be replaced by the vision of an indescribable tragedy, destruction, death! . . .

Marconigrams announced quickly to the world that a fatal wreck had taken place, that the giant of the Atlantic, like a wounded lion, bewailed its fate and the Hertzian waves scattered to the four points of the ocean's compass the cry of death of thousands of human beings who, with the "Titanic," were near sinking into the abyss of the great sea!

We don't wish to retrace here the sad story of the "Titanic," already too well known, but rather to consider some of the repercussions of this frightening maritime tragedy.

All the bourgeois journalists and hacks in this country, from the day of the disaster right to the present, have given the greater part of their columns to the sad story of the Titanic, have made and continue to make a world of chat, have cursed those responsible and called for new laws to guard (so they say) human life, and in a hundred articles have shown the heroism of Astor, Straus, Guggenheim, and other millionaires.

In all the churches of America sounds an echo of the press. The priests in their sermons portrayed with great pomposity the heroism of the rich, railing against the steamship company and invoking the law, seeing how invoking the good Lord was by now useless! . . .

And the legislators, too, were shaken up, and the sleeping U.S. Senate deemed it logical and proper to make a case of the White Star Line and its head, who saved himself by cunning or chance, nobody knows . . .

And what is all this uproar?

The answer is simple . . .

Among the dead were millionaires, and our readers have been able to read in other papers long articles and sensational stories about the 200 rich people, who with 1,400 poor, met their deaths, as if the heroism and the grief of the 1st, 2nd, and 3rd classes unfolded in the same circumstances! . . .

The crew, 700 in number, aware of their miserable fate, awaited death and like true martyrs to duty sank to the ocean depths with their ship; but concerning them the bourgeois press speaks of neither heroism nor sacrifice . . .

The emigrants, crammed in like transport merchandise, as numerous as the first class passengers, consigned to the bottom like bilge (many of whom were not even able to do anything in time to get out), were also heroes, but their heroism is of no consequence to the press, or the priests, or the bourgeoisie . . .

And today, today only, the bourgeoisie, itself stricken, speaks of laws *protective* of human life!

What irony!

In America 500,000 people are slaughtered in factories every year; they are workers, but neither the press, nor the priests, nor the senators are troubled about them. Sure: they are laborers and . . . it hardly matters!

Mining disasters take place every day and wreak destruction on the proletariat, but neither the press, nor the priests, nor the Senate pass new laws, nor initiate lawsuits—what do *miners* matter? Hundreds of thousands of them arrive every year from the Old World.

The Triangle Factory was an infernal trap and 147 girl workers were burnt to death. The ultra-guilty owners were pronounced innocent and set free by American judges. The venal press remains mute, the priests as silent as mummies, the senators sleep. Sure: they're the *people's* daughters . . . what do they matter?

One could go on a while, but to what advantage?

Cry, o wise ones; curse, irresponsible journalists; pray, priests: 5 or 6 million perish miserably, 5 or 6 bourgeois women are widowed . . .

Capitalism slaughters thousands and thousands of the proletariat every month, millions of women are left in mourning and misery, millions of children are left orphans, grieving and hungry. For them you have no pity, because you yourselves are the guilty ones. You do not curse their butchers, because they are you yourselves. You do not ask for new laws to guard the lives of these people, because they might harm your interests . . .

To all of you falls the blame for this continuing slaughter. You are guilty for this last and all the other disasters, because you uphold a society which considers profit more important than human life, and while today you grieve for the loss of members of your families, you should say *mea culpa!*

We, who struggle with every weapon at our disposal to overthrow the present social system, will avenge one day not too far distant all of your victims, including those of the "Titanic."

"The Titanic' Disaster and Peace,"
The Independent

EDWIN GINN (1838–1914)
Publisher, Philanthropist
June 13, 1912

I doubt if history records any nobler examples of heroism and self-sacrifice than were displayed by the passengers on board the steamship

"Titanic." The sole thought among the men was, "Are there any more women and children? If so, they must be cared for first." The question as to whether they were from the steerage or first cabin was not asked. No preference was shown. This should be a striking lesson to those who are constantly preaching the indifference of the rich to the condition of the poor.

Another great lesson to be drawn from this disaster is that bravery and heroism are not bred solely in battle. The men who sacrificed their lives at the sinking of this ship had been, for the most part, trained neither for the army nor the navy, yet they stood back calmly and courageously, knowing that death must certainly come in a few moments. The soldier in battle always feels that he has a chance of life, but the men on the "Titanic" knew that they were doomed.

During these days when the minds of all have been focused on this terrible tragedy I wonder how many have asked the question, Why is it that the world stands aghast at the loss of fifteen hundred souls, when the news of a battle in which twenty thousand men lie dead on the field and as many more are maimed for life excites so little comment? To be sure, many read the account with deep sorrow and regret, but it makes but a slight impression upon the community at large. None of the wheels of business is stopped; the churches hold no memorial services.

But hardly had the "Titanic" sank beneath the waves when the various steamship lines began to take measures to prevent, if possible, another such disaster. Orders were issued to have all passenger boats provided with enough lifeboats and rafts to accommodate every one on board; to install a sufficient number of wireless operators so that there would be always at his post an intelligent man familiar with the various codes; to lay out routes far enough south to avoid icebergs; to provide glasses for the lookout; to drill the crew daily in the performance of their duties. It should also be arranged that no man, captain or otherwise, would be obliged to be upon the bridge more than two nights in succession; and a rate of speed should be established, when in the vicinity of ice fields or in a fog, which would insure safety. Our Government, as well as the British Government, is investigating very carefully causes and conditions, and I hope that the maritime nations will in the near future enact laws which will insure the perpetuity of these safeguards by compelling their observance. The sinking of this great ship, with its precious freight of human life, will no doubt accomplish much in making ocean travel safe.

But what steps are being taken by the nations to save the world from a much greater sacrifice of human life in battle? And yet life should be as sacred in the one case as in the other. The only reason that I can see for the recognition of the value of human life in the one instance and its apparent disregard in the other is because of the feeling that one is an accident which should be avoided, while the other is taken as a matter of course, the result of many generations of custom and education. Men and women look upon the battlefield as a necessary evil, the only way in which the nations can be protected in their rights, and until they are brought to realize that human life should *always* be held sacred, we cannot hope to see the present war system done away with. Each nation is seeking its own interests, first, last, and all the time, rather than the good of all. This is a question that the individual nation can never settle. Efficient and resolute co-operation of all the nations is what we need.

In future conferences at The Hague for the discussion of these vital questions affecting international relations, I sincerely hope that the governments, backed by strong public opinion, will appoint only men of large scope and vision, who are capable of dissociating the selfish interests of their own nation from their considerations and are looking only to the benefit of the entire human race. I would take all such questions entirely out of the hands of military men. I do not desire to say anything deprecatory to those men in their place, for as a class they are as humane and noble as any others; but they are unconsciously influenced by their vocation and have no proper place in Hague conferences. In some nations it has been estimated that one-fifth or one-sixth of the entire population are pecuniarily interested in the continuance of the war system. In these conventions there should be no representative from any nation who is interested in such a system. The representatives should be those who have at heart the safety of the nations as a whole, and the creation of such a protective force as will insure the safety of each nation against the encroachment of any other. It would need but a very small proportion of the present armies and navies of the world to guarantee that protection. All of the instrumentalities necessary to carry on the world's work in peace and order would come naturally and easily after the rights of each nation have been secured in this way.

If these and similar lessons can be taken to heart in such a way as will bring about decisive action for the good of all, the heroes who were swept to their death on board the "Titanic" will not have given their lives in vain.

Letter to the Editor, The Baltimore Sun

W. LEVIN
April 20, 1912

Gallantry is an accomplishment that is considered part of the youthful training of our men today, but a very grave question has arisen as to whether such gallantry as that exhibited on board the ill-fated Titanic was fitting to the situation. We all realize that life is very sweet, even to the most lowly, but I cannot conceive how any captain can compare the life of such men as Astor, Straus, Butt and others to those of the lowly steerage passengers, simply because they were women.

When we look over the list we find among the missing men of our great financial world, whose endeavors have been from their youth to make this the greatest of all nations; men, who, by controlling large business interests, have been able to give hundreds of thousands employment; men whose fertile brains and active energy have risen to the highest pinnacle in their chosen professions, and we find such men compelled to stand aside by the captain's orders and go to their death because of the fact there were women in the steerage.

This foreign element, that demoralize whatever portion of any of our cities in which they happen to locate, are given the preference over men that a short time ago our nation was proud of. It may not sound altogether proper to speak of this matter as I do, but I firmly believe if a popular vote were taken on the question my opinion would lead by a big majority.

I will add in concluding that the newspapers cannot be too severe in their criticism of the White Star Line for its mysterious action in not giving the public the news of so terrible a disaster.

"Heroes Lay Down Their Lives That Others May Live," The Baltimore Sun

April 20, 1912

As though before them, in letters of fire, had flamed the words, "Greater love hath no man than this, that a man may lay down his life for his friend," the men, and even several women, died the death of true heroes on the ill-fated Titanic. The regal motto, "Noblesse Oblige," arose in more than one mind as some man of wealth and proud social standing gallantly stepped aside and gave his place to some unknown and poor unfortunate with a grace that could not be excelled in a ballroom.

But even above the other heroes stands out the figure of a Baltimore man, and to Howard B. Case was accorded the epitaph "The Big Hero of the Disaster." Mr. Case was the husband of former Miss Crowther, daughter of President John Crowther, of the Towson National Bank, and, with his wife, was accounted a resident of that suburb. Mr. Case instituted and supervised a system by which the women and children were transferred in safety to the small boats, and to his ingenuity and effort the safety of scores of lives is due.

And surely the mighty waves wash lightly over the form of Col. John Jacob Astor, who, favored with every blessing in life—a devoted young wife, an expected child and untold wealth at his command— counted all well lost that another might be saved and went to his fate like the true gentleman.

To Major "Archie" Butt, prime favorite of the President of the United States, no other death could have been more welcome than that through which he was enabled to save the life of a fellow-being. Even in the supreme moment, Major Butt stood the test, and his last act in this world was tenderly to place a woman in a lifeboat and send her on her fearsome way with words of encouragement and cheer.

Nor were the men alone in their heroism, and the name of Mrs. Isador Straus shines brightly against the black background of tragedy. "For better or for worse, in sickness and in death" had been the mutual pledge of Mrs. Straus and her sweetheart-husband, and to this she clung with unflinching devotion and refused to permit him to meet death alone. No more heart-moving sight can be pictured than that of this venerable, loving couple, going down to the depths of death together, entering the life everlasting with joy rather than misgiving.

Other heroes were there also, alas! unidentified. Their names will not be enrolled on the scroll of honor, but their gallant bravery shall not go unrewarded.

"Life is Cheap," The New Republic

WALTER LIPPMANN (1889–1974)
Journalist, Political Philosopher
December 19, 1914

When a military expert wishes to be very technical and professional he refers to the killed, wounded and missing as the wastage of an army. To those who do not share his preoccupation with the problems of grand strategy, the word connotes a cold and calculated horror based on a fatal disregard of human cost. It is natural, then, to fall back upon the old platitude that in war life is cheap; cheaper than guns, cheaper than dreadnoughts, cheaper even than intelligent diplomacy.

If we go behind this simple idea, however, we find curious distinctions reflected in ordinary feeling about the war. There was General Joffre's statement that the French would not waste men in furious assaults. In England this was received with approval, mixed with the feeling that the British were standing the worst of the racket. Most curious, however, was the English attitude towards the Russians. The Russians were conceived as an inexhaustible horde which could be poured endlessly against German guns. The value of individual Russians was ridiculously low as compared with individual Englishmen. In America the loss of two thousand Austrians would seem as nothing beside the loss of two thousand Englishmen. If the Canadians were to suffer heavily, we should feel it still more, no doubt.

When the *Titanic* sank, it was very noticeable that the anguish of the first-cabin passengers meant more to the newspapers than did that of the crew or steerage; and of the first-cabin passengers, it was the well-known people in whom was dramatized the full terror of the disaster. When a man is run over, the amount of space given to a report of the accident seems to depend very closely either on his social importance in the community, or on whether he is injured under circumstances which might apply to highly regarded elements of the population. The injuries of foreign-born laborers on construction work are hardly reported. It is estimated that one man is killed for every floor added to a skyscraper, but the fact does not rise to the level of popular interest. The value of a life seems to increase only as it emerges from a mass and becomes individualized. So long as great populations remain politically inert, so long as they can be treated in lumps, so long as they can be manipulated from above, they will be lightly used or easily disregarded.

It is in time of peace that the value of life is fixed. The test of war reveals it. That is why democracies tend to be peaceful. In them the importance of each person has been enlarged, and the greater the equality, the less able are small groups to use their fellows as brute instruments. Democracies are compelled to look toward peaceful adjustments because the cost of war is too tremendous for them. The mere fact that at a certain level of comfort and self-respect the birthrate declines makes the conservation of life imperative. It is in democracies based on fairly well distributed economic opportunity and a modicum of education that birth ceases to be a wholesale accident and becomes a considered purpose. France is such a democracy, and France does not spend life easily. The large measure of equality which she has achieved by a prudent birth-rate, a tolerable level of well-being, and a tradition of human rights, has made dreams of lavish conquest forever impossible to her. She will defend what she has with superb courage, but she cannot dominate the world.

There, perhaps, is the most important relation between social reform and the problem of peace. The aggressors of the future are likely to be the nations in which life is cheap, and the hope of international order rests with those countries in whom personality has become too valuable to be squandered. This is why the whole world waits the democratization of Germany, Russia and Japan.

But even the so-called democracies are far from a decent sense of the value of life. Here in America life is extraordinarily cheap. There is almost no task so dull, so degrading or so useless but you can find plenty of human beings to do it. You can hire a man to walk up and down the avenue carrying a sign which advertises a quack dentist. You can hire rows of men for the back line of the chorus, just standing them there to fill up space. You can hire a man to sit next to the chauffeur; he is called a footman and his purpose is to make the owner of the car a bit more comfortable and a great deal more magnificent. There are women known as lady's maids whose business it is to dress up other women. There are flunkeys whose mission it is to powder their hair, put on white stockings and gold-trimmed knee-breeches and flank the threshold of great houses. It is possible to hire any number of caretakers for empty houses, bellhops to fetch for you, even mourners to mourn for you.

Every city is full of women whose lives are gray with emptiness, who sit for hours looking out of the window, who rock their chairs and gossip, and long for the excitement that never comes. Unloved and unloving, and tragically unused, the world seems to have passed them by. Our cities are full of those caricatured homes, the close, curtained boarding houses to which people come from the day's drudgery to the evening's depression, the thousands of hall bedrooms in which hope dies and lives the ghost of itself in baseball scores and in movies, in the funny page and in Beatrice Fairfax,* in purchased romance and in stunted reflections of the music-hall.

It is not strange that in war we spend life so easily, or that our anxiety to lower the death-rate of babies, to keep the sick alive, to help the criminal and save the feeble-minded, seems to many a trifling human-

*Beatrice Fairfax, a pseudonym for Marie Manning (1873?–1945), was a popular columnist for the Hearst newspaper chain.

itarianism. The notion that every person is sacred, that no one is a means to some one else's end, this sentiment which is the heart of democracy, has taken only slight hold upon the modern world. It is still hardly questioned that men should die to protect concessions, to collect debts, to hold markets, to glorify their king, to avenge imaginary insults. In the industrial world men are used as "hands," kept waiting in idle crowds to fill casual jobs, put at work that exhausts and pays almost nothing, blocked in occupations from which they cannot learn, from which they become forever unfitted to escape. Women are used as drudges, as recreation, as things to jest about or to appropriate, because all through our civilization there runs an appalling insensitiveness and disregard. We have not yet made life dignified and valuable in itself, we have not yet made it a sufficient treasury of good things, have not infused it with the riches which men will not wantonly waste.

Human life will become valuable as we invest in it. The child that is worth bearing, nursing, tending and rearing, worth educating, worth making happy, worth building good schools and laying out playgrounds for, worth all the subtle effort of modern educational science, is becoming too valuable for drudgery, too valuable for the food of cannon. It is because for some years we have been putting positive values into life that this war appalls us more than it would have appalled our ancestors. And just so far as we can induce the state to sink money and attention in human beings, by just so much do we insure ourselves against idle destruction.

This is the best internal defense against those amongst us who may be dreaming of aggression. Every dollar and every moment of care devoted to increasing the individual importance of people, all skill and training, all fine organization to humanize work, every increase of political expression, is a protection against idle use of our military power, against any attempt to convert legitimate and necessary preparation for defense into an instrument of conquest. It may be said with justice that the man is dangerous who talks loudly about military preparation and is uninterested in social reform. It is the people engaged in adding to the values of civilization who have earned the right to talk about its defense.

"The Titanic," The Fra

ELBERT HUBBARD (1859–1915)
*Author, Lecturer, Founder of the Arts and Crafts Roycroft Shop,
Died on the* Lusitania
May 1912

It is a night of a thousand stars. The date, Sunday, April 14, 1912. The time, 11:20 P.M.

The place, off Cape Race—that Cemetery of the Sea.

Suddenly a silence comes—the engines have stopped—the great iron heart of the ship has ceased to beat.

Such a silence is always ominous to those who go down to the sea in ships.

"The engines have stopped!"

Eyes peer; ears listen; startled minds wait!

A half minute goes by.

Then the great ship groans, as her keel grates and grinds. She reels, rocks, struggles as if to free herself from a titanic grasp, and as she rights herself, people standing lose their center of gravity.

Not a shock—only about the same sensation that one feels when the ferryboat slides into her landing-slip, with a somewhat hasty hand at the wheel.

On board the ferry we know what has happened—here we do not.

"An iceberg!" someone cries.

The word is passed along.

"Only an iceberg! Barely grated it—side-swiped it—that is all! Ah, ha!"

The few on deck, and some of those in cabins peering out of portholes, see a great white mass go gliding by.

A shower of broken ice has covered the decks. Passengers pick up specimens "for souvenirs to carry home," they laughingly say.

Five minutes pass—the engines start again—but only for an instant.

Again the steam is shut off. Then the siren-whistles cleave and saw the frosty air.

Silence and the sirens! Alarm, but no tumult—but why blow the whistles when there is no fog!

The cold is piercing. Some who have come up on deck return to their cabins for wraps and overcoats.

The men laugh—and a few nervously smoke.

It is a cold, clear night of stars. There is no moon. The sea is smooth as a summer pond.

The great towering iceberg that loomed above the topmost mast has done its work, gone on, disappeared, piloted by its partners, the darkness and the night.

"There was no iceberg—you only imagined it," a man declares.

"Go back to bed—there is no danger—this ship cannot sink anyway!" says the managing director of the company.

In a lull of the screaming siren, a hoarse voice is heard calling through a megaphone from the bridge—"Man the lifeboats! Women and children first!"

"It sounds just like a play," says Henry Harris to Major Butt.

Stewards and waiters are giving out life-preservers and showing passengers how to put them on.

There is laughter—a little hysteria. "I want my clothes made to order," a woman protests. "An outrageous fit! Give me a man's size!"

The order of the captain on the bridge is repeated by other officers—"Man the lifeboats! Women and children first!"

"It's a boat-drill—that's all!"

"A precautionary measure—we'll be going ahead soon," says George Widener to his wife, in reassuring tones as he holds her hand.

Women are loath to get into the boats. Officers, not over-gently, seize them, and half lift and push them in. Children, crying, and some half asleep, are passed over into the boats.

Mother arms reach out and take the little ones. Parentage and ownership are lost sight of.

Some boats are only half filled, so slow are the women to believe that rescue is necessary.

The boats are lowered, awkwardly, for there has never been a boat drill, and assignments are being made haphazard.

A sudden little tilt of the deck hastens the proceeding. The bows of the ship are settling—there is a very perceptible list to starboard.

An Englishman, tired and blase, comes out of the smoking room, having just ceased a card game. He very deliberately approaches an officer who is loading women and children into a lifeboat.

The globe-trotting Briton is filling his pipe. "I si, orficer, you know; what seems to be the matter with this bloomin' craft, you know!"

"Fool," roars the officer, "the ship is sinking!"

"Well," says the Englishman, as he strikes a match on the rail, "Well, you know, if she is sinking, just let 'er down a little easy, you know."

John Jacob Astor half forces his wife into the boat. She submits, but much against her will. He climbs over and takes a seat beside her in the lifeboat. It is a ruse to get her in—he kisses her tenderly—stands up, steps lightly out and gives his place to a woman.

"Lower away!" calls the officer.

"Wait—here is a boy—his mother is in there!"

"Lower away!" calls the officer—"there is no more room."

Colonel Astor steps back. George Widener tosses him a woman's hat, picked up from the deck, Colonal Astor jams the hat on the boy's head, takes the lad up in his arms, runs to the rail and calls, "You won't leave this little girl, will you?"

"Drop her into the boat," shouts the officer. The child drops into friendly hands as the boat is lowered.

Astor turns to Widener and laughingly says, "Well, we put one over on 'em that time."

"I'll meet you in New York," calls Colonel Astor to his wife as the boat pulls off. He lights a cigarette and passes the silver case and a match box along to the other men.

A man runs back to his cabin to get a box of money and jewels. The box is worth $300,000. The man changes his mind and gets three oranges, and gives one orange each to three children as they are lifted into safety.

As a lifeboat is being lowered, Mr. and Mrs. Isador Straus come running with arms full of blankets, brought from their stateroom. They throw the bedding to the people in the boat.

"Help that woman in!" shouts an officer. Two sailors seize Mrs. Straus. She struggles, frees herself, and proudly says, "Not I—I will not leave my husband." Mr. Straus insists, quietly and gently, that she shall go. He will follow later.

But Mrs. Straus is firm. "All these years we have traveled together, and shall we part now? No, our fate is one."

She smiles a quiet smile, and pushes aside the hand of Major Butt, who has ordered the sailors to leave her alone. "We will help you—Ms. Straus and I—come! It is the law of the sea—women and children first—come!" said Major Butt.

"No, major; you do not understand. I remain with my husband— we are one, no matter what comes—you do not understand!"

"See," she cried, as if to change the subject, "there is a woman getting in the lifeboat with her baby; she has no wraps!"

Mrs. Straus tears off her fur-lined robe and places it tenderly around the woman and the innocently sleeping babe.

William T. Stead, grim, hatless, with furrowed face, stands with an iron bar in hand as a lifeboat is lowered. "Those men in the steerage, I fear, will make a rush—they will swamp the boats."

Major Butt draws his revolver. He looks toward the crowded steerage. Then he puts his revolver back into his pocket, smiles. "No, they know we will save their women and children as quickly as we will our own."

Mr. Stead tosses the iron bar into the sea.

He goes to the people crowding the afterdeck. They speak a polyglot language. They cry, they pray, they supplicate, they kiss each other in frenzied grief.

John B. Thayer, George Widener, Henry Harris, Benjamin Guggenheim, Charles M. Hays,* Mr. and Mrs. Straus, move among these people, talk to them and try to reassure them.

There are other women besides Mrs. Straus who will not leave their husbands.

These women clasp each other's hands. They smile—they understand!

Mr. Guggenheim and his secretary are in full dress. "If we are going to call on Neptune, we will go dressed as gentlemen," they laughingly say.

---

*John B. Thayer, vice-president of the Pennsylvania Railroad, Henry B. Harris, theatrical producer, and Charles M. Hays, president of the Grand Trunk Railroad, were first-cabin passengers.

The ship is slowly settling by the head.

The forward deck is below the water.

The decks are at a vicious angle.

The icy waters are full of struggling people.

Those still on the ship climb up from deck to deck.

The dark waters follow them, angry, jealous, savage, relentless.

The decks are almost perpendicular. The people hang by the rails.

A terrific explosion occurs—the ship's boilers have burst.

The last lights go out.

The great iron monster slips, slides, gently glides, surely, down, down, down into the sea.

Where once the great ship proudly floated, there is now a mass of wreckage, the dead, the dying, and the great black all-enfolding night.

Overhead, the thousand stars shine with a brightness unaccustomed.

The Strauses, Stead, Astor, Butt, Harris, Thayer, Widener, Guggenheim, Hays—I thought I knew you just because I had seen you, realized somewhat of your able qualities, looked into your eyes and pressed your hands, but I did not guess your greatness.

You are now beyond the reach of praise—flattery touches you not—words for you are vain.

Medals for heroism—how cheap the gilt, how paltry the pewter!

You are beyond our praise or blame. We reach out, we do not touch you. We call, but you do not hear.

Words unkind, ill-considered, were sometimes flung at you, Colonel Astor, in your lifetime. We admit your handicap of wealth— pity you for the accident of birth—but we congratulate you that as your mouth was stopped with the brine of the sea, so you stopped the months of the carpers and critics with the dust of the tomb.

If any think unkindly of you now, be he priest or plebeian, let it be with finger to his lips, and a look of shame into his own dark heart.

Also, shall we not write a postscript to that booklet on cigarettes?

Charles M. Hays you who made life safe for travelers on shore, yet you were caught in a sea-trap, which, had you been manager of that transatlantic line, would never have been set, baited as it was with human lives.

You placed safety above speed. You fastened your faith to utilities, not futilities. You and John B. Thayer would have had a searchlight and used it in the danger zone, so as to have located an iceberg five miles away. You would have filled the space occupied by that silly plunge bath (how ironic the thing) with a hundred collapsible boats, and nests of dories.

You, Hays and Thayer, believed in other men—you trusted them—this time they failed you. We pity them, not you.

And Mr. and Mrs. Straus, I envy you that legacy of love and loyalty left to your children and grandchildren. The calm courage that was yours all your long and useful career was your possession in death!

You knew how to do three great things—you knew how to live, how to love and how to die.

Archie Butt, the gloss and glitter on your spangled uniform were pure gold. I always suspected it.

You tucked the ladies in the lifeboats, as if they were going for an automobile ride. "Give my regards to the folks at home," you gaily called as you lifted your hat and stepped back on the doomed deck.

You died the gallant gentleman that you were. You helped preserve the old English tradition, "Women and children first."

All America is proud of you.

Guggenheim, Widener and Harris, you were unfortunate in life in having more money than we had. That is why we wrote things about you, and printed them in black and red. If you were sports, you were game to the last, cheerful losers, and all such are winners.

As your souls play hide-and-seek with sirens and dance with naiads, you have lost interest in us. But our hearts are with you still. You showed us how death and danger put all on a parity. The women in the steerage were your sisters—the men your brothers; and on the tablets of love and memory we have 'graved your names.

William T. Stead, you were a writer, a thinker, a speaker, a doer of the word. You proved your case; sealed the brief with your heart's blood; and as your bearded face looked in admiration for the last time up at the twinkling, shining stars, God in pardonable pride said to Gabriel, "Here comes a man!"

And so all you I knew, and all that thousand and half a thousand more, I did not know, passed out of this earth life into the unknown upon the unforgetting tide. You were sacrificed to the greedy Goddess of Luxury and her consort, the Demon of Speed.

Was it worth the while? Who shall say? The great lessons of life are learned only in blood and tears. Fate decreed that you should die for us.

Happily, the world has passed forever from a time when it feels a sorrow for the dead. The dead are at rest, their work is ended, they have drunk of the waters of Lethe, and these are rocked in the cradle of the deep. We kiss our hands to them and cry, "Hail and Farewell—until we meet again!"

But for the living who wait for a footstep that will never come, and all those who listen for a voice that will never more be heard, our hearts go out in tenderness, love and sympathy.

These dead have not lived and died in vain. They have brought us all a little nearer together—we think better of our kind.

One thing sure, there are just two respectable ways to die: One is of old age, and the other is by accident.

All disease is indecent.

Suicide is atrocious.

But to pass out as did Mr. and Mrs. Isador Straus is glorious. Few have such a privilege. Happy lovers, both. In life they were never separated, and in death they are not divided.

From a Speech, Charleston, West Virginia

MOTHER JONES (1843–1930)
Labor Activist
August 15, 1912

I have been reading of the *Titanic* when she went down. Did you read of her? The big guns wanted to save themselves, and the fellows that were guiding below took up a club and said we will save our people. And then the papers came out and said those millionaires tried to save the women. Oh, Lord, why don't they give up their millions if they want to save the women and children? Why do they rob them of home, why do they rob millions of women to fill the hell-holes of capitalism?

From *Wreck and Sinking of the Titanic*

MARSHALL EVERETT (HENRY NEIL) (1863–1939)
Author, Encyclopedist, Etiquette Expert
1912

Men whose names and reputation were prominent in two hemispheres were shouldered out of the way by roughly dressed Slavs and Hungarians. Husbands were separated from their wives in the battle to reach the boats. Tearful leave-takings as the lifeboats, one after another, were filled with sobbing women and lowered upon the ice-covered surface of the ocean were heart-breaking.

There was no time to pick or choose. The first woman to step into a lifeboat held her place even though she were a maid or the wife of a Hungarian peasant. Many women clung to their husbands and refused to be separated. In some cases they dragged their husbands to the boats and in the confusion the men found places in the boats.

"Lesson of the Titanic Disaster," The Public

LOUIS F. POST (1849–1928)
Newspaper Editor, Lawyer, Reformer, Assistant U.S. Secretary of Labor
April 1912

A tragedy so terrible and which might have been averted, naturally calls out bitter denunciations against the business men whose management is responsible. That all such denunciations, even the bitterest, are excusable in so far as they afford relief to overwrought sorrow or anger or horror, no one with a spark of the human in him would deny. That they are useful in so far as they tend to make ocean travel safer in the future, few would wish to dispute. But to all who have eyes to see or ears to hear, the "Titanic" disaster will carry a deeper lesson than the necessity for better safety appliances at sea; it will arouse higher emotions than anger at any person or class.

The inexcusable destruction of those fifteen hundred human lives was not all from greed. Though greed may have played a part along with many another impulse, it could have been only on the surface. Greed does not run deep. This was proved by the truest of tests at the climax of the tragedy. The democratic impulse—most distinctly human of all human characteristics, braver than greed and more absorbing than selfishness—came uppermost then. At that supreme moment, when human souls were on trial, the appeal to brotherhood was intuitive and overwhelming. Kiser's inspiring verse gives us the picture:

> Christian and Jew, and humble and high
> Master and servant, they stood at last,
> Bound by a glorious brotherly tie.

At last! But why only at last? Was the spirit of brotherhood absent before? Had greed crowded it out? Had consciousness of race or class made it insensible to every emotion but fear of death? This cannot be. Fear of death could not awaken a sense of brotherhood, fear of death could not make way for a democratic spirit to rise supreme—not if that sense, not if this spirit, were less powerful among human passions than selfishness. Were the democratic spirit indeed non-existent or paralyzed, were selfishness normally in supreme command, selfishness would be strengthened, not weakened, by fears of death and hopes of escape. No; not selfishness but democracy is the power that moves mankind at every crisis. Selfishness has no hold which the basic sense of democracy cannot loosen; none which it does not loosen in fact whenever the test comes. Yet there is an unhappy significance, unintended, it may be, but true, in Kiser's words—"at last." Is it only "at last," then, only when Death duels with Life, that the brotherly tie becomes the tie that binds, the democratic instinct the instinct that triumphs?

It may seem so. Daily tragedies to which the "Titanic" disaster is by comparison a trifling incident make it seem so. These tragedies are due to the laws under which we live; they are the frightful price that all have to pay for the luxury of some; but as to them, where is the brotherly inspiration to drive away greed, where the democratic instinct to dethrone the instinct of self love? Well may the question be asked, and hard enough may the finding of the answer be. But if the answer be hard to find, isn't it because it is so simple and so near—the pot of gold at the foot of the garden tree? Isn't it there in every human heart, but unawakened? If selfishness stubbornly prevails in the face of every-day industrial tragedies, may the reason not be that the philosophy of selfishness holds so many university chairs, is preached in thin spiritual disguise from so many pulpits, and gets tremendous emphasis in much socialist teaching, while so few stirring appeals are made to the great human instinct of democracy?

It cannot be from any lack of the democratic instinct that beneficiaries of privilege are selfishly indifferent to the heartsickening perennial tragedies of our industrial life. These folk are like all other folks; they have the same mixed impulses of selfishness, generosity and fairness. Not very different can any of them be from those of their own class who went down with the "Titanic." If they are careless of the awful industrial tragedies, or cold toward them, it must be because their democracy is not awakened. On that doomed vessel, along with their brethren of all classes there, those children of privilege, face to face with the tragic, were as democratic and as brave as any. But the industrial tragedies—these they do not feel, these they do not see, these are unreal to them, these they face, if they face them at all, only as conditions for charitable relief and not as preventable disasters of the social seas. The thrilling fact never stirs them, that they themselves flourish luxuriously upon the very tragedies that submerge their brethren in an ocean of servitude and poverty. What they lack is not democracy but imagination.

Let the privileged see the industrial tragedies they thrive upon, make them realize the tragical cost of their selfish luxury, and their icy greed will melt in the heat of their democracy. Real as their selfishness is, truly as it helps to make poverty and crime, it is no more basic or controlling with their class than with any other. Men of the kind who go bravely to death in sinking ships when rescue-appliances are inadequate for all, will as bravely give up their industrial privileges, once they understand that privilege for some spells disaster for others. Let their imaginations be fired, and they will feel their brotherhood and think of its responsibilities. Their sense of democracy will do the rest. And their imaginations can be fired, but not through calls to a war of classes, however peaceable in form. They must be fired by appeals to the democratic sense of brotherly rights and duties as opposed to undemocratic privilege and the unbrotherly classes that privilege produces.

From a Speech, Broadway Theater, New York

WILLIAM JENNINGS BRYAN (1860–1925)
Democratic Senator from Nebraska, Presidential Candidate, Secretary of State
April 21, 1912

A great emergency is like a stage upon which people play a part before an audience. As we walk the streets and meet people passing by, we cannot tell the hero from the villain. But when they come before us on the stage, they act out their parts and we can separate the one from the other.

And so these great emergencies try men's souls and they show us the little and the great. And this catastrophe has given the world the chance to see how many heroes there are who only need a call forward to vindicate their right to be admired.

A gentleman was telling me yesterday a story that he heard from one of the survivors. It was in that busy hour when all were seeking a means of escape. One of the passengers was putting on a life preserver, and said to the steward, "Where is yours?" He said, "There are not enough to go around." And he was doing what he could to help save the others.

And I am sure that none have read the story without being touched by it, of those wives who would not leave their husbands, who preferred to share the dangers of remaining than to seize the opportunity to escape.

I knew one of these men in Congress. I was a colleague of Mr.

Straus some twenty years ago, and it is pleasant to know that he was a hero and not afraid; and it is sweet to know that the wife who had been his companion for so many years was true to the history of an earlier Ruth, and preferred not to leave him—"Entreat me not to leave thee." These examples of manliness and womanliness are the heritage of our people. They make us proud of those whom we know, who are a part of us.

As to the future, nothing that we can say can bring back the dead. These occasions are for the future more than for now, for others more than for ourselves. Nearly thirty years ago I was talking in the street with a lawyer of Illinois City, and he referred to the Bible passage, "Without the shedding of blood there is no remission of sins." And he made an application of it that I had never heard before. He said: "You can't correct any great wrong till somebody's killed. You may talk to people about dangers, but they will not listen."

Often we do not know what needs to be done or provided until emergency throws its light upon the situation. Last November I was on a ship in the West Indies. At 3:45 o'clock in the morning it ran upon a coral reef, and for three hours our ship sat there, and we in darkness waited, not knowing how far it was to the nearest relief ship. I learned for the first time that they only had one wireless operator on ships of that size, and that by agreement the operators slept from 1:30 till 6 o'clock—four hours in the night when a sinking ship could not call another ship even if but a few miles away.

The moment we found out the situation we were all anxious that a law should be passed to require not less than two operators on a ship, that there might be no delay in the securing of succor. We were not in immediate danger, and we could wait for ten hours until a ship reached us. But in less than three hours the Titanic went down. We learned by experience that we needed more than one operator, and bills are now before Congress to remedy this, and I have no doubt that the result of this great disaster, this gigantic, this Titanic disaster, will result in legislation that will be beneficial to those who come after.

I venture the prediction that the wireless system will be made more immediately effective and efficient over a wider area; that better preparations will be made with lifeboats; that less attention will be paid to comforts, and more thought given to the lives of those intrusted to the care of these shipbuilders and ship owners. I venture to assert also that the mania for speed will receive a check, and that people will not be so anxious to get across the ocean in the shortest time as they are to get across.

From *"Some Aspects of the Admirable Inquiry,"* The English Review

JOSEPH CONRAD (1857–1924)
Author, Seaman
July 1912

I am not a soft-headed, humanitarian faddist. I have been ordered in my time to do dangerous work; I have ordered others to do dangerous work; I have never ordered a man to do any work I was not prepared to do myself. I attach no exaggerated value to human life. But I know it has a value for which the most generous contributions to the Mansion House and "Heroes" funds cannot pay. And they cannot pay for it, because people, even of the third class (excuse my plain speaking), are not cattle. Death has its sting. If Yamsi's* manager's head were forcibly held under the water of his bath for some little time, he would soon discover that it has. Some people can only learn from that sort of experience which comes home to their own dear selves.

I am not a sentimentalist; therefore it is not a great consolation to me to see all these people brevetted as "heroes" by the penny and half-penny Press. It is no consolation at all. In extremity, in the worst extremity, the majority of people, even of common people, will behave decently. It's a fact of which only the journalists don't seem aware. Hence their enthusiasm, I suppose. But I, who am not a sentimental-

---

*Yamsi, or Ismay spelled backwards, was the code name with which White Star Line Managing Director J. Bruce Ismay signed his messages informing the company of the disaster.

ist, think it would have been finer if the band of the *Titanic* had been quietly saved, instead of being drowned while playing—whatever tune they were playing, the poor devils. I would rather they had been saved to support their families than to see their families supported by the magnificent generosity of the subscribers. I am not consoled by the false, written-up, Drury Lane aspects of that event, which is neither drama, nor melodrama, nor tragedy, but an exposure of arrogant folly. There is nothing more heroic in being drowned very much against your will, off a holed, helpless, big tank in which you bought your passage, than in quietly dying of colic caused by the imperfect salmon in the tin you bought from your grocer.

And that's the truth. The unsentimental truth stripped of the romantic garment the Press has wrapped around this most unnecessary disaster.

"The Titanic: Some Unmentioned Morals," The Daily News

GEORGE BERNARD SHAW (1856–1950)
Playwright, Fabian Socialist
May 14, 1912

Why is it that the effect of a sensational catastrophe on a modern nation is to cast it into transports, not of weeping, not of prayer, not of sympathy with the bereaved nor congratulations of the rescued, not of poetic expression of the soul purified by pity and terror, but of a wild defiance of inexorable Fate and undeniable Fact by an explosion of outrageous romantic lying?

What is the first demand of romance in a shipwreck? It is the cry of Women and Children First. No male creature is to step into a boat as long as there is a woman or child on the doomed ship. How the boat is to be navigated and rowed by babies and women occupied in holding the babies is not mentioned. The likelihood that no sensible woman would trust either herself or her child in a boat unless there was a considerable percentage of men on board is not considered. Women and children first: that is the romantic formula. And never did the chorus of solemn delight at the strict observance of this formula by the British heroes on board the *Titanic* rise to sublimer strains than in the papers containing the first account of the wreck by a surviving eye witness, Lady Duff Gordon.* She described how she escaped in the captain's boat. There was one other woman in it, and ten men: twelve all told. One woman for every five men. Chorus: "Not once or twice in our rough island story," etc., etc.

Second romantic demand. Though all the men (except the foreigners, who must all be shot by stern British officers in attempting to rush the boats over the bodies of the women and children) must be heroes, the captain must be a super-hero, a magnificent seaman, cool, brave, delighting in death and danger, and a living guarantee that the wreck was nobody's fault, but, on the contrary, a triumph of British navigation. Such a man Captain Smith was enthusiastically proclaimed on the day when it was reported (and actually believed, apparently) that he had shot himself on the bridge, or shot the first officer, or been shot by the first officer, or shot anyhow to bring the curtain down effectively. Writers who had never heard of Captain Smith to that hour wrote of him as they would hardly write of Nelson. The one thing positively known was that Captain Smith had lost his ship by deliberately and knowingly steaming into an ice field at the highest speed he had coal for. He paid the penalty; so did most of those for whose lives he was responsible. Had he brought them and the ship safely to land, nobody would have taken the smallest notice of him.

Third romantic demand. The officers must be calm, proud, steady, unmoved in the intervals of shooting the terrified foreigners. The verdict that they had surpassed all expectations was unanimous. The actual evidence was that Mr. Ismay was told by the officer of his boat to go to hell, and that boats which were not full refused to go to the rescue of those who were struggling in the water in cork jackets. Reason

---

*First-cabin passenger Lucile Duff Gordon was a famous dress designer. She and her husband, Sir Cosmo Duff Gordon, escaped with ten others in a lifeboat designed to carry forty.

frankly given: they were afraid. The fear was as natural as the officer's language to Mr. Ismay: who of us at home dare blame them or feel sure that we should have been any cooler or braver? But is it necessary to assure the world that only Englishmen could have behaved so heroically, and to compare their conduct with the hypothetic dastardliness which lascars or Italians or foreigners generally—say Nansen or Amundsen or the Duke of Abruzzi—would have shown in the same circumstances?

Fourth romantic demand. Everybody must face death without a tremor; and the band, according to the *Birkenhead* precedent, must play "Nearer, my God, to Thee," as an accompaniment to the invitation to Mr. Ismay to go to hell. It was duly proclaimed that thus exactly it fell out. Actual evidence: the captain and officers were so afraid of a panic that, though they knew the ship was sinking, they did not dare to tell the passengers so—especially the third-class passengers—and the band played RagTimes to reassure the passengers, who, therefore, did not get into the boats, and did not realise their situation until the boats were gone and the ship was standing on her head before plunging to the bottom. What happened then Lady Duff Gordon has related, and the witnesses of the American inquiry could hardly bear to relate.

I ask, What is the use of all this ghastly, blasphemous, inhuman, braggartly lying? Here is a calamity which might well make the proudest man humble, and the wildest joker serious. It makes us vainglorious, insolent, and mendacious. At all events, that is what our journalists assumed. Were they right or wrong? Did the Press really represent the public? I am afraid it did. Churchmen and statesmen took much the same tone. The effect on me was one of profound disgust, almost of national dishonour. Am I mad? Possibly. At all events, that is how I felt and how I feel about it. It seems to me that when deeply moved men should speak the truth. The English nation appears to take precisely the contrary view. Again I am in the minority. What will be the end of it?—for England, I mean. Suppose we came into conflict with a race that had the courage to look facts in the face and the wisdom to know itself for what it was. Fortunately for us, no such race is in sight. Our wretched consolation must be that any other nation would have behaved just as absurdly.

"Mr. Shaw and the Titanic," The Daily News

ARTHUR CONAN DOYLE (1859–1930)
Author
May 20, 1912

I have just been reading the article by Mr. Bernard Shaw upon the loss of the *Titanic,* which appeared in your issue of May 14th. It is written professedly in the interests of truth, and accuses everyone around him of lying. Yet I can never remember any production which contained so much that was false within the same compass. How a man could write with such looseness and levity of such an event at such a time passes all comprehension.

Let us take a few of the points. Mr. Shaw wishes—in order to support his perverse thesis, that there was no heroism—to quote figures to show that the women were not given priority in escape. He picks out, therefore, one single boat, the smallest of all, which was launched and directed under peculiar circumstances, which are now matter for inquiry. Because there were ten men and two women in this boat, therefore there was no heroism or chivalry; and all talk about it is affectation. Yet Mr. Shaw knows as well as I know that if he had taken the very next boat he would have been obliged to admit that there were 65 women out of 70 occupants, and that in nearly all the boats navigation was made difficult by the want of men to do the rowing. Therefore, in order to give a false impression, he has deliberately singled out one boat; although he could not but be aware that it entirely misrepresented the general situation. Is this decent controversy, and has the writer any cause to accuse his contemporaries of misstatement?

His next paragraph is devoted to the attempt to besmirch the conduct of Capt. Smith. He does it by his favourite method of "suggestio falsi"—the false suggestion being that the sympathy shown by the public for Capt. Smith took the shape of condoning Capt. Smith's navigation. Now everyone—including Mr. Bernard Shaw—knows perfectly well that no defence has ever been made of the risk which was run, and that the sympathy was at the spectacle of an old and honoured sailor who has made one terrible mistake, and who deliberately gave his life in reparation, discarding his lifebelt, working to the last for those whom he had unwillingly injured, and finally swimming with a child to a boat into which he himself refused to enter. This is the fact, and Mr. Shaw's assertion that the wreck was hailed as a "triumph of British navigation" only shows—what surely needed no showing—that a phrase stands for more than truth with Mr. Shaw. The same remark applies to his "wrote of him as they would hardly write of Nelson." If Mr. Shaw will show me the work of any responsible journalist in which Capt. Smith is written of in the terms of Nelson, I will gladly send £100 to the Fabian Society.

Mr. Shaw's next suggestion—all the more poisonous because it is not put into so many words—is that the officers did not do their duty. If his vague words mean anything they can only mean this. He quotes as if it were a crime the words of Lowe* to Mr. Ismay when he interfered with his boat. I could not imagine a finer example of an officer doing his duty than that a subordinate should dare to speak thus to the managing director of the Line when he thought that he was impeding his life-saving work. The sixth officer went down with the captain, so I presume that even Mr. Shaw could not ask him to do more. Of the other officers I have never heard or read any cause for criticism. Mr. Shaw finds some cause for offence in the fact that one of them discharged his revolver in order to intimidate some foreign immigrants who threatened to rush the boats. The fact and the assertion that these passengers were foreigners came from several eye witnesses. Does Mr. Shaw think it should have been suppressed? If not what is he scolding about?

Finally, Mr. Shaw tries to defile the beautiful incident of the band by alleging that it was the result of orders issued to avert panic. But if it were, how does that detract either from the wisdom of the orders or from the heroism of the musicians? It was right to avert panic, and it was wonderful that men could be found to do it in such a way.

As to the general accusation that the occasion has been used for the glorification of British qualities, we should indeed be a lost people if we did not honour courage and discipline when we see it in its highest form. That our sympathies extend beyond ourselves is shown by the

---

*Fifth Officer Harold Godfrey Lowe.

fact that the conduct of the American male passengers, and very particularly of the much-abused millionaires, has been as warmly eulogised as any single feature in the whole wonderful epic.

But surely it is a pitiful sight to see a man of undoubted genius using his gifts in order to misrepresent and decry his own people, regardless of the fact that his words must add to the grief of those who have already had more than enough to bear.

"The Age of Chivalry," *Editorial,*
The Tampa Tribune

April 22, 1912

Amidst the din of "votes for women," the clamor and the window-smashing, we frequently hear that "the age of chivalry is dead."

"Let us have the suffrage," they say; woman is no longer deferred to. What we want is the ballot, never mind the gallantry; give us our rights and we will take care of the rest."

And yet the age of chivalry is not dead, says the Savannah Press. Nearly every woman on the steamship Titanic when the time came to fill the lifeboats were given the preference, and rowed to a place of safety. It was a British ship filled with English and Americans. These are countries where the window-smashing and the clamor most abound, and yet when the tumult of the shouting died we have the record of more than seventy-five per cent of women passengers, first class, intermediate and steerage, rescued by the gallant men or given places in the life-boats to the exclusion of the male passengers, who met death without a murmur.

Speculators have spun favorite theories that in this practical working world women have lost their place and forfeited the sweet courtesy, the undisputed precedence which has been the time honored right of the eternal feminine. Acting upon this, some women have mounted the rostrums and called for the suffrage as the only safeguard which will protect her and vindicate her. And yet when the men on the Titanic, with the chivalry of the "knights of old" were called upon to stand back and make way for the women, they bowed in ancient courtesy and saluted the departing life-boats with a God's speed worthy of their lineage. There was no line of caste; steerage and saloon passengers observed the same rules and saw their women carried to safety through the ice-packed waters toward the lights of the Carpathia. The next short-haired suffragette who shouts defiance on the stump and clings to the ballot as the only safeguard in a world where men and women are crowding the decks and calling for lifelines, should remember the picture of the Titanic. If not her hearers should recall it for her.

For, after all, it isn't the vote a woman needs, adds the Press. It is her own personality, her gentleness, her sex. Sometimes her very dependence enhances her charm and increases her chances in life. The other day a prominent citizen of Savannah had a call from a woman who laid before him a proposition and insisted that it be considered upon its cold business merits. The gentleman considered it and promptly turned it down. Then the canvasser made an appeal to him as a woman. His sympathies were touched, his chivalrous nature responded, and he accepted her proposition without a question. Better woman's undisputed sphere than "seek for rule, supremacy and sway."

"*Suffrage and Life-Saving,*" The Woman's Journal

ALICE STONE BLACKWELL (1857–1950)
Suffragist, Reformer, Editor
April 27, 1912

An effort is being made in some quarters to deduce from the wreck of the Titanic an argument against votes for women. Now we have chivalry, and if we had votes, we are told, chivalry would be destroyed. There never was a clearer proof that the question who shall be saved first at sea has nothing to do with the ballot. Most of the Titanic's crew had no votes. Some of the women were voters, like Mrs. J. J. Brown* of Denver, who rowed one of the boats for seven hours, encouraging and cheering up the survivors, and showing chivalry herself to those less courageous than herself. In the famous Birkenhead disaster, the soldiers who stood fast in their ranks on the deck of the sinking ship were vote-less men. It is absurd to fancy that chivalry is a tribute rendered by a voter to a non-voter as a sort of offset for the lack of the ballot.

The special agent of the Chinese Merchants' Association is quoted as saying: "It is the duty of sailors, when a Chinese vessel goes down, to save men first, children next, and women last. This is on the theory that men are most valuable to the State." This rule, existing for centuries in a country where women have been kept in extreme subjection, is actually brought forward by an Anti in the New York Evening Post as having some connection with the recent granting of woman suffrage in the Chinese republic!

Others say the manifestation of chivalry on the Titanic shows that women do not need a vote—chivalry is enough. But the "law of the sea" is quite different from the custom on land. The captain is expected to be the last man to leave his ship; all other lives must be saved before his. The captain of industry makes sure first of a comfortable living for himself, even if the workers in his employ die of tuberculosis through insufficient food and unsanitary conditions. The chivalry shown to a few hundred women on the Titanic does not alter the fact that in New York City 150,000 people—largely women and children—have to sleep in dark rooms with no windows; that in a single large city 5,000 white slaves die every year; that the lives and health of thousands of women and children are sacrificed continually through their exploitation in mills, workshops and factories. These things are facts.

The wreck of the Titanic was due to the reckless and unrestrained commercialism which too largely rules the world today, and which woman suffrage, we believe, will tend to mitigate. Women bring men into the world; they know the cost of human life: and when they have a voice in shaping legislation, they will provide for more adequate safe-

---

*First-cabin passenger Margaret Tobin Brown, "the Unsinkable Molly Brown."

guards and precautions. There was no need that a single life should have been lost upon the Titanic. There will be far fewer lost by preventable accidents, either on land or sea, when the mothers of men have the right to vote.

Letter to the Editor, The Baltimore Sun

H. C. MESSERLR
April 24, 1912

Reading over the various letters in your paper, I find that I can't entertain the opinion that the lives of Colonel Astor and Major Butt should not have been sacrificed to save some poor, ignorant immigrant woman, who could do no more good to our country than to bring a number of laborers into this world. If she has done so, she has performed her real object in coming into this world, and in the eyes of her Creator is of greater value than she, perhaps, of society, who does not. Indeed, we naturally say to ourselves, looking back to the Titanic disaster, we would much have preferred to have such men as Astor, Straus and Butt living. But in dying as heroes, as they did, they are of far greater value to their country in the fine example they set of heroism and love to the weaker and lower ranks of man than all their millions or reputation of wealth could have done.

What a shame it would have been to pick out some few passengers simply on account of their wealth and like cowards crush back and trample over some poor beings who, perhaps, were less fortunate in obtaining wealth, but whose character and manhood was unspotted! A catastrophe such as this one is very much like the calling of the final trumpet. The Lord will make no distinction of persons and neither should we.

In a case like this the question as to who is of greater usefulness to our country cannot be considered. The women were not saved because the crew considered them of greater value to mankind, but merely out of inborn respect to woman as the weaker sex.

Let the suffragists remember this. When the Lord created woman and placed her under the protection of man he had her well provided for. The Titanic disaster proves it very plainly. All honor to the victims of that disaster, especially to such of the wealth or reputation of Colonel Astor, Isidor Straus and Major Butt.

Letter to the Editor, The Baltimore Sun

"DAUGHTER OF EVE"
May 1, 1912

I have noted the letter of H. C. Messerlr, of Concord, N.C., in your issue of April 24. I have no comments to make as to the heroism of the men on the Titanic who gave up their places to women in the lifeboats. As to how much of this heroism was due to the belief in the unsinkable qualities of the ship, or what part pistols played in converting cowards into brave men, I have nothing to say. These men have paid the biggest price that one can be called upon to pay—the yielding up of their lives—and we mourn for them and will remember them as heroes.

But I have something to say concerning Mr. Messerlr's statement that "when the Lord created woman and placed her under the protection of man, He had her well provided for." The following are some of the laws that have been framed by men and are upon the statute books of most of our States: (1) Fathers disposing absolutely of the children the women have borne. (2) Failure to protect girls by fixing the age of consent in tender years, with leniency toward unchaste men. (3) Unequal divorce laws, the husband legally able to divorce his wife for unfaithfulness only, while the wife must prove extreme cruelty in addition to unfaithfulness. (4) The widow having to divide her husband's property with his family, but the widower receiving the entire estate of his wife. (5) The father inheriting the entire property of an intestate unmarried child, the mother getting nothing. Are we to accept these laws as bearing out the testimony of your correspondent that the protection of women by men is all that could be asked for or desired?

"A Man's View," Letter to the Editor,
The St. Louis Post-Dispatch

W. C. RICKSTER
April 26, 1912

I have never been a woman's rights man. I have always claimed that a woman could get her rights—man's, too—and if there is anything left she can get that, too, if she knows how to go about it. When everything else fails she has her persuasive powers that makes the miser buy her sealskin coats, diamonds and fancy hats. I suggest, henceforth, when a woman talks woman's rights, she be answered with the word Titanic, nothing more—just Titanic.

"Lives Against Lives," The Woman's Journal

AGNES E. RYAN (1878–1954)
Suffragist, Reformer
April 27, 1912

Not many times in every-day American history-in-the-making is the nation stirred out of its ordinary trend. Last week was an exception. Millions were thrilled and stirred to the depths by the report that sixteen hundred men and women were waked from their sleep at midnight to learn that they were sinking 2,000 fathoms deep to the bottom of the ocean, entombed in the steamship Titanic.

After the first shock of the awful news, the practical American began to ask questions: "Could this appalling disaster have been prevented?" "How was the vessel equipped?" "Who was to blame?" "Were all precautions taken?" "Is this such a disaster as must be expected at sea?" The nation is stirred, and official investigation is started. It is a sea tragedy the like of which has not been known!

Some rather startling and damaging facts seem about to be established:

1. On the one hand, the Titanic was the newest and largest ocean liner in the world. Her fatal trip was her maiden trip. She had cost over $5,000,000 in building. She was supposed to have the newest and best equipment that science and invention and human skill could devise. She had many luxurious appointments for the comfort and amusement of her passengers.

2. On the other hand, she was not fitted with the equipment necessary to safe-guard the life of either her crew or her passengers. For instance, she did not carry enough life boats to save all on board. Her lookout man was not provided with a marine glass. She carried no searchlight. Her wireless service was totally inadequate. Her crew were not drilled in the use of life boats.

When asked by the investigating committee this week if it was not true that the Titanic had only about half enough life appliances for the people on board, one of the ship's surviving officers answered, "Yes, sir, but she complied with all the British requirements."

In this one sentence is established the connection between this kind of disaster and the Votes for Women movement. For after all, whether such disasters shall befall us or not is a simple matter of laws and the enforcement of laws. Therefore, while the laws and the enforcement of the laws are entirely in men's hands, these wholesale, life-taking disasters must almost be expected. Dollars and cents are put over against humanity and life itself in equipping our monstrous vessels. Everything is done to make and equip a vessel that will attract patronage. But in safe-guarding the lives of those it has enticed on board, there is no marine glass, no searchlight, only half enough life boats and inadequate wireless service; a boy of 22 is employed to operate the wireless at $20 a month, while another vessel has no night shift in its wireless service at all!

It simmers down, then, to the usual story of life and death, dollars and cents, law and the enforcement of law. The difference is that it is a vessel at sea at midnight with 1,600 lives lost by foundering instead of a factory here and there burning a hundred girls alive, or a mine smothering its hundreds to death, or the railroads sacrificing their thousands.

The need of women in all departments of human life to conserve life itself is pitiful. More than anything else in the world the Votes for Women movement seeks to bring humaneness, the valuation of human life, into the commerce and transportation and business of the world and establish things on a new basis, a basis in which the unit of measurement is life, nothing but life!

Sixteen hundred people, full of hopes and plans, trusted their lives to a vessel equipped and inspected by the British government. Two weeks have scarcely passed and they lie smothered in a sunken vessel, or their lifeless bodies float on the troubled waters!

> "Ye banks and braes o'bonnie Doon,
>   How can ye bloom sae fresh and fair,
> How can ye chant, ye little birds,
>   And I sae weary, full o' care?"

To the woman-heart of the nation this is not a tragedy to mourn and grieve over and forget; it is simply typical of the countless lives that perish needlessly each year from the Ship of State! It gives new proof that the State needs women in law-making and law-enforcing, and it gives new impetus to the Votes for Women movement.

"Masculine Chivalry," Progressive Woman

May 1912

When the great steamer Titanic went down recently it carried with it something like 1,500 human beings, the great majority of them men. Reports have it that about 800 women and children were saved, and something like 80 men, besides the sailors who manned the lifeboats.

We know that these women and children were saved because the men stood back and—gave their lives instead. That is a terrible test of "chivalry" at a time like this. Men who feel themselves of importance in the world of affairs, step aside and give unknown women and children precedence in a life-and-death test.

We are filled with something akin to awe when we think of the personal struggles that must have filled each breast as its owner watched his last hope of life slipping away from him, saw some frail woman taking his place in the lifeboats, and felt the darkness closing in about him.

But they did it. And yet most of those men, no doubt, stubbornly opposed the idea of the rights of women in participation in governmental affairs. Exploited them in industry, voted for the white slave pen, sent the daughter to the street, the son to the army, the husband to tramp the streets for a job! Four hundred immigrant women were saved. What of the lives of these poor women once they reach New York?

It is a strange situation, and one which no doubt requires the deep and unfathomable processes of the masculine brain to account for. No woman has yet been able to understand it. And, if you please, the women are beginning to say they are willing to exchange the chivalry for the right to help run a government that will build safer ships, safer mines and mills and factories, establish more departments for human welfare and think less of the profits and the gaudy display of the few at the cost of so many lives.

Chivalry, no doubt, has its attractive, romantic side, but just plain common sense would serve social progress so much better!

"The Anglo-Saxon Ideal," Editorial,
Temperance Educational Quarterly

July 1912

That there is a law stronger than the statute law has been clearly revealed by the fateful disaster of the Titanic. The Anglo-Saxon ideal was asserted when the life-boats which at best could hold but one-third of those in peril were held for the women and the children.

"Women and children first," said the ship's officers and men.

"Women and children first," said the heroic men passengers who stood back and helped the women and the children into the boats.

"Women and children first" was the ideal firmly established when fourteen hundred men met death in the icy waters.

A sublime ideal remains the same in whatever region or circumstances in which it may be found. And on the land, in days of peace and security, surely the ideal still stands true—women and children first. In the planning of the home, in the planning of the state, in the planning of the life of the nation, the same kind of heroism as shown on the Titanic says, "women and children first." It is as true today as it ever was, that

" 'Tis man's pride,

His highest, worthiest, noblest boast,

The privilege he prizes most,

To stand by helpless woman's side."

and to place her and his children first in all that he plans to do.

What relation has this great Anglo-Saxon ideal to the temperance problem or to the liquor traffic? In considering the sale of strong drink with its physical and moral effects, do men say, "women and children first?"

How does the sale of strong drink affect the women and the children for whom the heroic men on board the Titanic gladly died? From every corner of the universe comes the reply, *"the women and the children are the chief sufferers from the sale of liquor."*

Every woman who marries has the right to happiness which is never concommitant with the use of liquor. Every child has the right to be well born. Frances E. Willard* said:

"Of all the laws I can think of, I hold in highest dignity and most awful significance the laws of the descent of inheritance, of parental

---

*Frances E. Willard (1839–1898) was the first secretary and later president of the Women's Christian Temperance Union and the first president of the National Council of Women.

influences, of the determining of destiny before a soul has known an independent heart-beat or an intelligent volition. I hold that all reforms have their root here, and that a wiser and more thoughtful age, not very far distant, will stand aghast as it reads of the present dance of delirium and death with respect to the right of any child to be well born."

In considering the sale of liquor, not self-gratification, or personal liberty, or anything of the sort will appeal to the man with the true ideal, the ideal that was proclaimed forever to be the ideal of the Anglo-Saxon race, when on the sinking Titanic, men said, "Women and children first."

From *Sinking of the Titanic and Great Sea Disasters*

LOGAN MARSHALL
1912

Somewhere in the shadow of the appalling *Titanic* disaster slinks—still living by the inexplicable grace of God—a cur in human shape, to-day the most despicable human being in all the world.

In that grim midnight hour, already great in history, he found himself hemmed in by the band of heroes whose watch word and countersign rang out across the deep—"Women and children first!"

What did he do? He scuttled to the stateroom deck, put on a woman's skirt, a woman's hat and a woman's veil, and picking his crafty way back among the brave and chivalric men who guarded the rail of the doomed ship, he filched a seat in one of the life-boats and saved his skin.

His name is on that list of branded rescued men who were neither picked up from the sea when the ship went down nor were in boats under orders to help them safe away. His identity is not yet known, though it will be in good time. So foul an act as that will out like murder.

The eyes of strong men who have read this crowded record of golden deeds, who have read and re-read that deathless roll of honor of the dead, are still wet with tears of pity and of pride. This man still lives. Surely he was born and saved to set for men a new standard by which to measure infamy and shame.

"On the Sea of Life," The Denver Post

May 1, 1912

Icebergs are a dreadful danger in the "lanes" across which the transatlantic liners make their way. They are dangers difficult to detect. To avoid them the liner must steer a longer and more difficult course, and her officers must exercise ceaseless vigilance. So in the course which the young man takes on the sea of life. The career-wrecking icebergs of Indifference and Dissipation are likely to drift across his path. If he does not take the more arduous "lane"—the longer but safer course; if he does not keep a vigilant lookout; does not stay in charge upon the bridge of the good ship Self—wreck is inevitable. And the ocean of Failure is very deep.

"The Nobility of Self-Sacrifice," The New Orleans Times-Picayune

April 26, 1912

It takes great disasters to bring out in their finest colors the highest qualities of human nature. It is in the supreme moments of life that the true man or woman displays those splendid attributes which verify the Biblical claim that God made man after his own image. While the frightful wreck of the Titanic developed many heroes and countless acts of fortitude and self-sacrifice, the beautiful devotion displayed by Mrs. Isidor Strauss [sic] in firmly refusing to take her place with other women in the lifeboats and electing to remain by the side of her husband to share with him the fate that at the moment was inevitable, transcends all else. Mrs. Strauss is reported as saying that she had lived happily with her husband for nearly half a century, and, therefore, saw no reason why she should not remain by his side to the end. It is no wonder that this beautiful picture of wifely devotion, incomparable in its pathos and unique in its tragic surroundings, has enthused the entire world.

In this day of frequent and scandalous divorces, when the marriage tie once held so sacred is all too lightly regarded, the wifely devotion and love of Mrs. Strauss for her partner of a lifetime stands out in noble contrast. The world needed a reminder that married love and devotion cannot be cast off like a worn garment and that there are still married couples who never allow their early love to grow cold with the passing of time. Mrs. Strauss' devotion to her partner of a lifetime is a powerful rebuke to the hundreds and thousands of men and women who have lightly put aside for trivial cause, or no cause at all, the partners they vowed to love and protect while life should last. To such the beautiful picture of Mrs. Strauss electing to remain and die with her aged partner is a condemnation too pointed to be misunderstood.

There are without doubt hundreds of thousands of couples who live happily together as did Mr. and Mrs. Strauss, and who would under similar circumstances elect to die together rather than be parted, but the evil of divorce and the conspicuous part which divorced people have played in our social life in recent years divert the popular mind from the contemplation of old-fashioned marital devotion. It required such a conspicuous exhibition that conjugal affection and devotion still existed among us as that given by Mr. and Mrs. Strauss to revive faith in the virtue and constancy of men and women. Mrs. Isidor Strauss' display of wifely love and devotion, even unto death, is a stronger sermon on the sacredness of the marriage tie than any the most distinguished divine could preach.

"The Saving of Women in Disaster,"
The Forerunner

CHARLOTTE PERKINS GILMAN (1860–1935)
Feminist, Author, Editor
May 1912

The world-grieving loss of the Titanic, with its splendid record of human heroism, has roused some comment as to the saving of women at the sacrifice of men. The natural base of this custom lies in the value of motherhood. In overcrowded countries, like China, different standards prevail. Races of the Teutonic and Scandinavian stocks, which rose from the matriarchal state without a period of polygamy and woman slavery, have the tradition of "chivalry" and uphold it in many respects. The courageous and self-sacrificing men who gave up their lives to save women are to be honored truly, but so should we honor the women who waive this sex advantage and choose to die like brave and conscientious human beings, rather than live on a wholly feminine basis. In all that pain and grief and courage one bit of snobbery stands out—among those saved from death we find Mrs. So and So "and maid"! Had the "maid" no name, no anxious relatives?

"Suffrage Dealt Blow by Women of Titanic,"
The Denver Post

EMMA GOLDMAN (1869–1940)
Anarchist, Feminist
April 21, 1912

Barring all sensational and conflicting reports of the Titanic horrors there are two features which seem to have been overlooked altogether. One is, the part woman has played in the terrible disaster, which to say the least, is in keeping with centuries of her training as a mere female.

With all the claims the present-day woman makes for her equality with man, her great intellectual and emancipatory achievements, she continues to be as weak and dependent, as ready to accept man's tribute in time of safety and his sacrifice in time of danger, as if she were still in her baby age.

"The men stood aside to let the ladies go first!" What about the ladies? What about their love superior to that of the men? What about their greater goodness? Their demand to equal rights and privileges? Is this to be found only at the polls, or on the statutes? I fear me very much that the ladies who have so readily accepted the dictations of the men, who stood by when the men were beaten back from the life-boats, have demonstrated their utter unfitness and inferiority, not merely to the title of man's equal, but to her traditionary fame of goodness, love and self-sacrifice.

It is to be hoped that some there were among the steerage victims at least, who preferred death with those they loved to life at the expense of the loved ones.

The second feature is this: To die for those we love is no small matter in a world where each is for himself and the devil take the hindmost. But to die for those far removed from us by a cold and cruel social and material gulf—for those who by their very position must needs be our enemies—for those who, a few moments before the disaster probably never gave a thought to the toilers and pariahs of the ship—is so wonderful a feat of human nature as to silence forever the ridiculous argument against the possibilities of human nature. The average philistine forever prates of how human nature must be coerced and beaten; how it must be kept in check and disciplined. How little he knows of the grandeur of human nature has never before been so magnificently demonstrated as by the crew of the Titanic, the sailors, stokers, workers, and drones belonging to the disinherited of the earth!

With neither club or statute to compel them, I wonder what induced these men to go to their death with greater fortitude than do soldiers on the battlefield? Why, it is human nature, stripped of all social artifice, of the deadening and dulling chase for material gains. Human nature, come into its own! Into its deep social kinship which so far has only expressed itself in great stress but which points to still greater possibilities for the future, when man shall no longer his brother maim!

From *The Loss of the SS Titanic*

LAWRENCE BEESLEY (1877–1967)
Teacher, Titanic *Survivor*
1912

It is a pitiful thing to recall the effects of sending down the first boats half full. In some cases men in the company of their wives had actually taken seats in the boats—young men, married only a few weeks and on their wedding trip—and had done so only because no more women could then be found; but the strict interpretation by the particular officer in charge there of the rule of "Women and children only," compelled them to get out again. Some of these boats were lowered and reached the Carpathia with many vacant seats. The anguish of the young wives in such circumstances can only be imagined. In other parts of the ship, however, a different interpretation was placed on the rule, and men were allowed and even invited by officers to get in—not only to form part of the crew, but even as passengers. This, of course, in the first boats and when no more women could be found.

The varied understanding of this rule was a frequent subject of discussion on the Carpathia—in fact, the rule itself was debated with much heart-searching. There were not wanting many who doubted the justice of its rigid enforcement, who could not think it well that a husband should be separated from his wife and family, leaving them penniless, or a young bridegroom from his wife of a few short weeks, while ladies with few relatives, with no one dependent upon them, and few responsibilities of any kind, were saved. It was mostly these ladies who pressed this view, and even men seemed to think there was a good deal to be said for it. Perhaps there is, theoretically, but it would be impossible, I think, in practice. To quote Mr. Lightoller* again in his evidence before the United States Senate Committee,—when asked if it was a rule of the sea that women and children be saved first, he replied,

---

*Second Officer Charles Herbert Lightoller.

"No, it is a rule of human nature." That is no doubt the real reason for its existence.

But the selective process of circumstances brought about results that were very bitter to some. It was heartrending for ladies who had lost all they held dearest in the world to hear that in one boat was a stoker picked up out of the sea so drunk that he stood up and brandished his arms about, and had to be thrown down by ladies and sat upon to keep him quiet. If comparisons can be drawn, it did seem better that an educated, refined man should be saved than one who had flown to drink as his refuge in time of danger.

These discussions turned sometimes to the old enquiry—"What is the purpose of all this? Why the disaster? Why this man saved and that man lost? Who has arranged that my husband should live a few short happy years in the world, and the happiest days in those years with me these last few weeks, and then be taken from me?" I heard no one attribute all this to a Divine Power who ordains and arranges the lives of men, and as part of a definite scheme sends such calamity and misery in order to purify, to teach, to spiritualize. I do not say there were not people who thought and said they saw Divine Wisdom in it all,—so inscrutable that we in our ignorance saw it not; but I did not hear it expressed, and this book is intended to be no more than a partial chronicle of the many different experiences and convictions.

There were those, on the other hand, who did not fail to say emphatically that indifference to the rights and feelings of others, blindness to duty toward our fellow men and women, was in the last analysis the cause of most of the human misery in the world. And it should undoubtedly appeal more to our sense of justice to attribute these things to our own lack of consideration for others than to shift the responsibility on to a Power whom we first postulate as being All-wise and All-loving.

All the boats were lowered and sent away by about 2 A.M., and by this time the ship was very low in the water, the forecastle deck completely submerged, and the sea creeping steadily up to the bridge and probably only a few yards away.

"Titanic Talk Dupes Man,"
The Chicago Tribune

April 24, 1912

F. J. Sansinger of Springfield, O., reported to the police last night that he had been swindled out of $50 by two confidence men. While waiting for a train, he said, he was accosted by a man who posed as a stranger. The latter suggested a walk to the lake front, where, he said, they could view the work on a ship to be constructed to represent the sunken Titanic. After a walk of several blocks down the lake front Sansinger's comrade suggested they match pennies with $1 bills as the stakes. The two were approached by a man claiming to be a detective, who said he was going to arrest them for gambling. Sansinger, acting on advice of his companion, paid the "detective" $50 for his release.

"Remembering Marconi," Editorial,
The Atlanta Constitution

April 19, 1912

Outstanding in the Titanic disaster is the heroism that gives the lie to the croak of decay in the human race. The Anglo-Saxon may yet boast that his sons are fit to rule the earth so long as men choose death with the courage they must have displayed when the great liner crashed into the mountain of ice, and the aftermath brought its final test. When that is said, it remains that the women and children snatched from the maw of the sea owe their lives to Guglielmo Marconi, the Italian inventor of wireless telegraphy.

Had it not been for the invisible waves pulsing out from the stricken vessel and imploring aid, there would probably not have been one survivor to tell the tale of the world's greatest marine disaster. It is true that the lifeboats would have been heavy with their burden of human freight. But expert testimony is to the effect that the hardiest man could not have survived the polar temperature that prevailed in the ice-pack that jostled these frail crafts. It was the Carpathia, striding up at top-speed in answer to the wireless summons, that took women, children and men from the tumbling lifeboats and cheated the sea of further toll. Had the Parisian and the Virginian, which also caught the call, been swifter ships or nearer the scene of disaster, it is conceivable that not one life would have been forfeit.

There is somber, unspeakable tragedy enough in the thing as it is. The sudden drama out on the broad Atlantic will take a sufficient tribute in seared lives and broken bones. But for the practical magic of the Italian, the terror of the tale would have been intensified. To the brave men—humble and great—who found deep-sea sepulcher would be added the women and little children for whose lives these men so blithely surrendered their own.

Editorial, The St. Paul Appeal

April 20, 1912

The most gigantic marine disaster in history, the sinking of the Titanic early Monday morning, has filled the civilized world with sorrow and horror. It proves the fallacy of "unsinkable (?)" ships just as several horrible fires showed the fallacy of fireproof buildings. It also showed how the safe-guarding of human lives is so frequently almost overlooked in the desire for luxury, elegance and speed in common carriers in this get-rich-quick age. And now that the horse has escaped we will see all sorts of attempts to close the stable door, and laws will be passed which, if complied with, another such disaster cannot soon again occur. And, while the whole world is lauding the men on the ship for their heroism in their "Women and children first" martyrdom, we can claim a few of the heroes, as the Afro-American must have been represented, as he generally is, in everything in this country. And though the daily press has made no special mention of him, we know he was there, and that he died like the other men. And we shed tears to his memory as well as to the men of other nationalities who died with him. And when in the last day the sea gives up its dead, he, like the others, will come into his crown of glory.

From *The Truth About the Titanic*

ARCHIBALD GRACIE (1859–1912)
Army Officer, Historian, Titanic *Survivor*
1913

My energies were so concentrated upon this work of loading the boats at this quarter that lapse of time, sense of sight and sense of hearing recorded no impressions during this interval until the last boat was lowered; but there is one fact of which I am positive, and that is that every man, woman, officer and member of the crew did their full duty without a sign of fear or confusion. Lightoller's strong and steady voice rang out his orders in clear firm tones, inspiring confidence and obedience. There was not one woman who shed tears or gave any sign of fear or distress. There was not a man at this quarter of the ship who indicated a desire to get into the boats and escape with the women. There was not a member of the crew who shirked, or left his post. The coolness, courage, and sense of duty that I here witnessed made me thankful to God and proud of my Anglo-Saxon race that gave this perfect and superb exhibition of self-control at this hour of severest trial. "The boat's deck was only ten feet from the water when I lowered the sixth boat," testified Lightoller, "and when we lowered the first, the distance to the water was seventy feet." We had now loaded all the women who were in sight at that quarter of the ship, and I ran along the deck with Clinch Smith* on the port side some distance aft shouting, "Are there any more women?" "Are there any more women?" On my return there

*First-cabin passenger J. Clinch Smith.

was a very palpable list to port as if the ship was about to topple over. The deck was on a corresponding slant. "All passengers to the starboard side," was Lightoller's loud command, heard by all of us. Here I thought the final crisis had come, with the boats all gone, and when we were to be precipitated into the sea.

Prayerful thoughts now began to rise in me that my life might be preserved and I be restored to my loved ones at home. I weighed myself in the balance, doubtful whether I was thus deserving of God's mercy and protection. I questioned myself as to the performance of my religious duties according to the instructions of my earliest Preceptor, the Rev. Henry A. Coit, whose St. Paul's School at Concord, N.H., I had attended. My West Point training in the matter of recognition of constituted authority and maintenance of composure stood me in good stead.

Editorial, The Pittsburgh Courier

April 27, 1912

The Negroes who consider their poverty a curse may find consolation in the fact that they were not wealthy enough to take passage on the Titanic. Every adversity has its virtue.

"Editorial Notes," The New York Age

April 25, 1912

There may have been a negro in the sinking of the great steamship Titanic, off the Newfoundland coast last week, but the newspapers have not as yet discovered the fact. It is rather remarkable that there could be so great a tragedy without a negro somewhere concealed or exposed in it.

From *Sinking of the Titanic and Great Sea Disasters*

LOGAN MARSHALL
1912

An hour later, when the second wireless man came into the boxlike room to tell his companion what the situation was, he found a negro stoker creeping up behind the operator and saw him raise a knife over his head. He said afterwards—he was among those rescued—that he realized at once that the negro intended to kill the operator in order to take his life-belt from him. The second operator pulled out his revolver and shot the negro dead.

"What was the trouble?" asked the operator.

"That negro was going to kill you and steal your life-belt," the second man replied.

"Thanks, old man," said the operator. The second man went on deck to get some more information. He was just in time to jump overboard before the *Titanic* went down. The wireless operator and the body of the Negro who tried to steal his belt went down together.

From an *Editorial,* The Philadelphia Tribune

April 27, 1912

We thought it would be strange if there were no coloured persons aboard the fated ship. Of course, he had to be made to appear in the light of a dastard.

"Crazed by Wreck Talk," The New York Times

April 18, 1912

Atlantic City, N.J., April 17.—Crazed by brooding over the Titanic disaster, Joseph Fisher of this city last night became violently insane. He was taken to the County Asylum after a struggle with half a dozen policemen.

Although Fisher had neither friends nor relatives aboard the wrecked liner, he eagerly read all the news concerning the deaths of the victims. He became violent as he discussed the failure of the life-saving outfit of the liner to rescue all the passengers. Physicians fear that he never will recover.

"Reads of Titanic Disaster; Crazed; Wades Into Lake," The Chicago Tribune

April 22, 1912

James O'Hara, formerly a bell boy at the Auditorium hotel and believed to have been mentally unbalanced by reading of the Titanic disaster, marched out into the lake at the foot of Foster avenue yesterday afternoon, waving a long saber.

"No ship leaves the shore," he announced. "I am a-gonta stop these shipwrecks."

Patrolmen Ericson and Moyer started to wade into the icy water after him, but withdrew when the water rose over their shoes. They decoyed him ashore, then took him to the detention hospital.

"He Was Driven Insane by the Titanic Tragedy," The Atlanta Constitution

April 23, 1912

Sharon, Pa., April 22.—John M. Smith, of Hickory Township, a former sailor, became violently insane last night after reading accounts of the disaster to the Titanic. Smith had walked several miles to get newspapers containing the news.

"Crazed by Fancied Horrors," The New York Times

April 19, 1912

Since reading the first news of the sinking of the Titanic, Philip Terretsky, 27 years old, of 235 East Thirteenth Street, has been distressed by thoughts of what the passengers endured, and early yesterday morning he became hysterical.

Terretsky has been haunted night and day by visions of imaginary scenes on the liner. Shortly after midnight, his roommate, Ryman Soloman, was awakened by Terretsky, who became so excited that Soloman called in Patrolman McHugh, who summoned Dr. Sovak from Bellevue. For an hour the surgeon treated the young man and finally quieted him with opiates.

"Wreck Causes Rich Woman to Throw Self Into Ocean," The Denver Post

April 20, 1912

Santa Monica, Cal., April 20.—The body of Mrs. M. U. Scuehler, said to have been a wealthy woman of St. Louis, Mo., was found in the ocean here today. She had jumped to her death some time last night.

According to friends, Mrs. Scuehler was much affected by the accounts of the Titanic disaster, and it is believed that her mind gave way.

"Editor Killed in Office," The Baltimore Sun

April 25, 1912

Spokane, Wash., April 24.—E. H. Rothrock, city editor of the Spokane Chronicle, was shot and killed today in the Chronicle editorial rooms by Richard Aleck, a Russian laborer.

Aleck first told the police he had been on the Titanic and then that he had been on the Carpathia, and mumbled "there had been too much printed about the disaster." He would give no other reason for the crime.

Aleck walked into the Chronicle local editorial room and asked for the editor. As Rothrock walked toward him Aleck drew a revolver and shot him in the breast. Rothrock died within five minutes.

The murderer later told the police that he was 40 years old and came to this country four years ago.

"Hurt in Argument About the Titanic,"
The St. Louis Post-Dispatch

April 22, 1912

An argument over the sinking of the Titanic resulted in Martin Kistener, 32 years old, of 211 Miller street, going to the observation ward of the city hospital, where he was Monday, with a lacerated scalp.

Kistener says he was in a bootblack stand at Broadway and Merchant street Sunday, when he became involved in the argument. Another man, he says, hit him on the head with a beer bottle, remarking he would "show him how the iceberg sank the Titanic."

August Besch, 219 Miller street; Rudolph Hicks, 802 Ann avenue and Edward Walton, 1504 South Eleventh street, are held pending investigation.

From *A Night to Remember*

WALTER LORD (1917–)
Historian
1955

As the sea closed over the *Titanic,* Lady Cosmo Duff Gordon in Boat I remarked to her secretary Miss Francatelli, "There is your beautiful nightdress gone."

A lot more than Miss Francatelli's nightgown vanished that April night. Even more than the largest liner in the world, her cargo, and the lives of 1502 people.

Never again would men fling a ship into an ice field, heedless of warnings, putting their whole trust in a few thousand tons of steel and rivets. From now on Atlantic liners took ice messages seriously, steered clear, or slowed down. Nobody believed in the "unsinkable ship."

Nor would icebergs any longer prowl the seas untended. After the *Titanic* sank, the American and British governments established the International Ice Patrol, and today Coast Guard cutters shepherd errant icebergs that drift toward the steamer lanes. The winter lane itself was shifted further south, as an extra precaution.

And there were no more liners with only part-time wireless. Henceforth every passenger ship had 24-hour radio watch. Never again could the world fall apart while a Cyril Evans* lay sleeping off-duty only ten miles away.

It was also the last time a liner put to sea without enough lifeboats. The 46,328-ton *Titanic* sailed under hopelessly outdated safety regulations. An absurd formula determined lifeboat requirements: all British vessels over 10,000 tons must carry 16 lifeboats with a capacity of 5500 cubic feet, plus enough rafts and floats for 75 per cent of the capacity of the lifeboats.

For the *Titanic* this worked out at 9625 cubic feet. This meant she had to carry boats for only 962 people. Actually, there were boats for 1178—the White Star Line complained that nobody appreciated their thoughtfulness. Even so, this took care of only 52 per cent of the 2207 people on board, and only 30 per cent of her total capacity. From now on the rules and formulas were simple indeed—lifeboats for everybody.

And it was the end of class distinction in filling the boats. The White Star Line always denied anything of the kind—and the investigators backed them up—yet there's overwhelming evidence that the steerage took a beating: Daniel Buckley kept from going into First Class . . . Olaus Abelseth released from the poop deck as the last boat pulled away . . . Steward Hart convoying two little groups of women topside, while hundreds were kept below . . . steerage passengers crawling along the crane from the well deck aft . . . others climbing vertical ladders to escape the well deck forward.

Then there were the people Colonel Gracie, Lightoller and others

*Evans was the wireless operator on the *Californian*, a ship said to have been within rescue distance of the *Titanic*.

saw surging up from below, just before the end. Until this moment Gracie was sure the women were all off—they were so hard to find when the last boats were loading. Now, he was appalled to see dozens of them suddenly appear. The statistics suggest who they were—the *Titanic's* casualty list included four of 143 First Class women (three by choice) . . . 15 of 93 Second Class women . . . and 81 of 179 Third Class women.

Not to mention the children. Except for Lorraine Allison, all 29 First and Second Class children were saved, but only 23 out of 76 steerage children.

Neither the chance to be chivalrous nor the fruits of chivalry seemed to go with a Third Class passage.

It was better, but not perfect, in Second Class. Lawrence Beesley remembered an officer stopping two ladies as they started through the gate to First Class. "May we pass to the boats?" they asked.

"No, madam; your boats are down on your own deck."

In fairness to the White Star Line, these distinctions grew not so much from set policy as from no policy at all. At some points the crew barred the way to the Boat Deck; at others they opened the gates but didn't tell anyone; at a few points there were well-meaning efforts to guide the steerage up. But generally Third Class was left to shift for itself. A few of the more enterprising met the challenge, but most milled helplessly about their quarters—ignored, neglected, forgotten.

If the White Star Line was indifferent, so was everybody else. No one seemed to care about Third Class—neither the press, the official Inquiries, nor even the Third Class passengers themselves.

In covering the *Titanic,* few reporters bothered to ask the Third Class passengers anything. The New York *Times* was justly proud of the way it handled the disaster. Yet the famous issue covering the *Carpathia's* arrival in New York contained only two interviews with Third Class passengers. This apparently was par for the course—of 43 survivor accounts in The New York *Herald,* two again were steerage experiences.

Certainly their experiences weren't as good copy as Lady Cosmo Duff Gordon (one New York newspaper had her saying, "The last voice I heard was a man shouting, 'My God, My God!' "). But there was indeed a story. The night was a magnificent confirmation of "women and children first," yet somehow the loss rate was higher for Third Class children than First Class men. It was a contrast which would never get by the social consciousness (or news sense) of today's press.

Nor did Congress care what happened to Third Class. Senator Smith's *Titanic* investigation covered everything under the sun, including what an iceberg was made of ("Ice," explained Fifth Officer Lowe), but the steerage received little attention. Only three of the witnesses were Third Class passengers. Two of these said they were kept from going to the Boat Deck, but the legislators didn't follow up. Again, the testimony doesn't suggest any deliberate hush-up—it was just that no one was interested.

The British Court of Enquiry was even more cavalier. Mr. W. D. Harbinson, who officially represented the Third Class interests, said he could find no trace of discrimination, and Lord Mersey's report gave a clean bill of health—yet not a single Third Class passenger testified, and the only surviving steward stationed in steerage freely conceded that the men were kept below decks as late as 1:15 A.M.

Even the Third Class passengers weren't bothered. They expected class distinction as part of the game. Olaus Abelseth, at least, regarded access to the Boat Deck as a privilege that went with First and Second Class passage . . . even when the ship was sinking. He was satisfied as long as they let him stay above decks.

A new age was dawning, and never since that night have Third Class passengers been so philosophical.

At the opposite extreme, it was also the last time the special position of First Class was accepted without question. When the White Star Liner *Republic* went down in 1908, Captain Sealby told the passengers entering the lifeboats, "Remember! Women and children go first; then the First Cabin, then the others!" There was no such rule on the *Titanic*, but the concept still existed in the public mind, and at first the press tended to forestall any criticism over what a First Class passenger might do. When the news broke that Ismay was saved, the New York *Sun* hastened to announce, "Ismay behaved with exceptional gallantry . . . no one knows how Mr. Ismay himself got into a boat; it is assumed he wished to make a presentation of the case to his company."

Never again would First Class have it so good. In fact, almost immediately the pendulum swung the other way. Within days Ismay was pilloried; within a year a prominent survivor divorced her husband merely because, according to gossip, he happened to be saved. One of the more trying legacies left by those on the *Titanic* has been a new standard of conduct for measuring the behavior of prominent people under stress.

It was easier in the old days ... for the *Titanic* was also the last stand of wealth and society in the center of public affection. In 1912 there were no movie, radio or television stars; sports figures were still beyond the pale; and café society was completely unknown. The public depended on socially prominent people for all the vicarious glamour that enriches drab lives.

This preoccupation was fully appreciated by the press. When the *Titanic* sailed, the New York *Times* listed the prominent passengers on the front page. After she sank, the New York *American* broke the news on April 16 with a lead devoted almost entirely to John Jacob Astor; at the end it mentioned that 1800 others were also lost.

In the same mood, the April 18 New York *Sun* covered the insurance angle of the disaster. Most of the story concerned Mrs. Widener's pearls.

Never again did established wealth occupy people's minds so thoroughly. On the other hand, never again was wealth so spectacular. John Jacob Astor thought nothing of shelling out 800 dollars for a lace jacket some dealer displayed on deck when the *Titanic* stopped briefly at Queenstown. To the Ryersons there was nothing unusual about traveling with 16 trunks. The 190 families in First Class were attended by 23 handmaids, eight valets, and assorted nurses and governesses— entirely apart from hundreds of stewards and stewardesses. These personal servants had their own lounge on C Deck, so that no one need suffer the embarrassment of striking up a conversation with some handsome stranger, only to find he was Henry Sleeper Harper's dragoman.

Or take the survivors' arrival in New York. Mrs. Astor was met by two automobiles, carrying two doctors, a trained nurse, a secretary and Vincent Astor. Mrs. George Widener was met not by automobile but by a special train—consisting of a private Pullman, another car for ballast, and a locomotive. Mrs. Charles Hays was met by a special train too, including two private cars and two coaches.

It was a reception in keeping with people who could afford as much as 4350 dollars—and these were 1912 dollars—for a de-luxe suite. A suite like this had even a private promenade deck, which figured out at something like 40 dollars a front foot for six days.

This kind of life, of course, wasn't open to everybody—in fact it would take Harold Bride, who made 20 dollars a month, 18 years to earn enough to cross in style—so those who enjoyed it gradually became part of a remarkably tightly-knit little group, which also seemed to vanish with the *Titanic*.

There was a wonderful intimacy about this little world of the Edwardian rich. There was no flicker of surprise when they bumped into each other, whether at the Pyramids (a great favorite), the Cowes Regatta, or the springs at Baden-Baden. They seemed to get the same ideas at the same time, and one of these ideas was to make the maiden voyage of the largest ship in the world.

So the *Titanic*'s trip was more like a reunion than an ocean passage. It fascinated Mrs. Henry B. Harris, wife of the theatrical producer, who certainly wasn't part of this world. Twenty years later she still recalled with awe, "There was a spirit of camaraderie unlike any I had experienced on previous trips. No one consulted the passenger list, to judge from the air of good fellowship that prevailed among the cabin passengers. They met on deck as one big party."

This group knew the crew almost as well as each other. It was the custom to cross with certain captains rather than on particular ships, and Captain Smith had a personal following which made him invaluable to the White Star Line. The Captain repaid the patronage with little favors and privileges which kept them coming. On the last night John Jacob Astor got the bad news direct from Captain Smith before the general alarm, and others learned too.

But the other end of the bargain was to respect the privilege. Nobody took advantage of the Captain's confidence—hardly a man in the group was saved.

The stewards and waiters were on equally close terms with the group. They had often looked after the same passengers. They knew just what they wanted and how they liked things done. Every evening Steward Cunningham would enter A-36 and lay out Thomas Andrews' dress clothes just the way Mr. Andrews liked. Then at 6:45 Cunningham would enter and help Andrews dress. It happened all over the ship.

And when the *Titanic* was going down, it was with genuine affection that Steward Etches made Mr. Guggenheim wear his sweater . . . that Steward Crawford laced Mr. Stewart's shoes . . . that Second Steward Dodd tipped off John B. Thayer that his wife was still on board, long after Thayer thought she had left. In the same spirit of devotion, Dining Room Steward Ray pushed Washington Dodge into Boat 13—he had persuaded the Dodges to take the *Titanic* and now felt he had to see them through.

The group repaid this loyalty with an intimacy and affection they gave few of their less-known fellow passengers. In the *Titanic's* last hours men like Ben Guggenheim and Martin Rothschild seemed to see more of their stewards than the other passengers.

The *Titanic* somehow lowered the curtain on this way of living. It never was the same again. First the war, then the income tax, made sure of that.

With this lost world went some of its prejudices—especially a firm and loudly voiced opinion of the superiority of Anglo-Saxon courage. To the survivors all stowaways in the lifeboats were "Chinese" or "Japanese"; All who jumped from the deck were "Armenians," "Frenchmen," or "Italians."

"There were various men passengers," declared Steward Crowe at the U. S. inquiry, "probably Italians, or some foreign nationality other than English or American, who attempted to rush the boats." Steward Crowe, of course, never heard the culprits speak and had no way of knowing who they were. At the inquiry things finally grew so bad that the Italian Ambassador demanded and got an apology from Fifth Officer Lowe for using "Italian" as a sort of synonym for "coward."

In contrast, Anglo-Saxon blood could do no wrong. When Bride described the stoker's attack on Phillips, some newspapers made the stoker a Negro for better effect. And in a story headlined, "Desirable Immigrants Lost," the New York *Sun* pointed out that, along with the others, 78 Finns were lost who might do the country some good.

But along with the prejudices, some nobler instincts also were lost. Men would go on being brave, but never again would they be brave in quite the same way. These men on the *Titanic* had a touch—there was something about Ben Guggenheim changing to evening dress . . . about Howard Case flicking his cigarette as he waved to Mrs. Graham . . . or even about Colonel Gracie panting along the decks, gallantly if ineffectually searching for Mrs. Candee. Today nobody could carry off these little gestures of chivalry, but they did that night.

An air of *noblesse oblige* has vanished too. During the agonizing days of uncertainty in New York, the Astors, the Guggenheims and others like them were not content to sit by their phones or to send friends and retainers to the White Star Line offices. They went themselves. Not because it was the best way to get information, but because they felt they ought to be there in person.

Today families are as loyal as ever, but the phone would probably do. Few would insist on going themselves and braving the bedlam of the steamship office. Yet the others didn't hesitate a minute. True, Vincent Astor did get better information than the rest—and some even spoke to General Manager Franklin himself—but the point is that these people didn't merely keep in touch—they were *there*.

Overriding everything else, the *Titanic* also marked the end of a general feeling of confidence. Until then men felt they had found the answer to a steady, orderly, civilized life. For 100 years the Western world had been at peace. For 100 years technology had steadily improved. For 100 years the benefits of peace and industry seemed to be filtering satisfactorily through society. In retrospect, there may seem less grounds for confidence, but at the time most articulate people felt life was all right.

The *Titanic* woke them up. Never again would they be quite so sure of themselves. In technology especially, the disaster was a terrible blow. Here was the "unsinkable ship"—perhaps man's greatest engineering achievement—going down the first time it sailed.

But it went beyond that. If this supreme achievement was so terribly fragile, what about everything else? If wealth meant so little on this cold April night, did it mean so much the rest of the year? Scores of ministers preached that the *Titanic* was a heaven-sent lesson to awaken people from their complacency, to punish them for top-heavy faith in material progress. If it was a lesson, it worked—people have never been sure of anything since.

The unending sequence of disillusionment that has followed can't be blamed on the *Titanic,* but she was the first jar. Before the *Titanic,* all was quiet. Afterward, all was tumult. That is why, to anybody who lived at the time, the *Titanic* more than any other single event marks the end of the old days, and the beginning of a new, uneasy era.

There was no time for such thoughts at 2:20 A.M., Monday, April 15, 1912. Over the *Titanic's* grave hung a thin, smoky vapor, soiling the clear night. The glassy sea was littered with crates, deck chairs, planking, pilasters, and corklike rubbish that kept bobbing to the surface from somewhere now far below.

"*THS Surpasses 1,000-Member Mark,*"
The Titanic Commutator

December 1975

Quietly and without editorial fanfare in local newspapers, radio, or television, history has been made. During the month of October, 1975, those who formed what is now known as the TITANIC HISTORICAL SOCIETY realized another dream-come-true. This organization has, at last, surpassed the 1,000-member mark. Interest in the history of the TITANIC and her sister-ships is now more than evident by those who continue to join our club in increasing numbers and by supporters who continue to maintain their memberships year after year.

In 1963, the society then known as the TITANIC ENTHUSI-ASTS of AMERICA, banded together to "... perpetuate and investigate the memory and history of the TITANIC and her sister-ships as well as the White Star Line ..." and total supporters at that time were a mere hand-full of Active members (the founding fathers) and the balance comprising of Honor members (made up largely of survivors of the TITANIC disaster of 1912). Presently, in the Fall of 1975, we have more than 950+ Active, dedicated members in the society, while the rest of the club's roster is comprised of Honor, Associate and Contributing memberships.

How coincidental it was too that one of our new members joining in the Active member roster during October was none other than a 17-year-old Spring City, Pennsylvania native who recently reigned as queen at homecoming festivities at Owen J. Roberts High School. Her name is Barbara M. Titanic, and it is thanks to THS Active Member, Arnie Watson of Pottstown, Pennsylvania, who submitted Miss Titanic's membership.

It is interesting to note the different feelings of THS founders and present officers of the society at this stage. Mr. Bob Gibbons of Missouri reflects, ". . . Well we have now achieved another milestone in our club's history. It is really gratifying to know that so many people out there share the same interests that we do. It makes it worth all the effort that we put into the organization." Bill Tantum of Connecticut made his feelings known by stating, "I believe in this society. We have helped to make available to its members various pieces of history that they could not otherwise obtain and thanks to the increasing number of members more of this historic material can be had and preserved." Tantum was referring to the many reprint books of 1912 volumes that have been obtained through 7C's Press, among them being, THE TRUTH ABOUT THE TITANIC, by Archibald Gracie, THE LOSS OF THE TITANIC by Lawrence Beesley, both survivors of the TITANIC, along with numerous other books and pamphlets that 7C's has made available to the members. Jack Eaton of New York spoke of the name change of the club that took place in 1974 and thought that the new name would better signify the organization's goals.

For Ed. Kamuda of Indian Orchard it is something else. "The members of this society are fabulous people," he says, "their support, both physical and financial is second to none. I can remember all the trouble we went through to interest model companies to market a TITANIC model . . . all thought that there was no market for it. Our members disagreed. Along came Entex Industries in 1973 and here we are two years later with a tremendous model kit which our members are buying and their praise for this project, along with helpful suggestions on improving the quality of the model are most commendable. Through Vantage Recording of Pennsylvania, a special TITANIC record was introduced and thanks to the support of our members, the project was a tremendous success. But what impressed me most was the meeting in Greenwich, Connecticut in 1973 when our society celebrated its Tenth Anniversary. Here was history in the making and the comments made there by those who attended indicated a deep and genuine 'feeling' for the TITANIC and her history. More important was the general view by members of our organization, who believe that our society holds an integral part in the continuing of the history of the former White Star liner."

What about the future of the society? The general opinion of THS officers indicates a rather optimistic forecast. The ultimate goal is two-fold: one has to do with the creation of a THS museum to house artifacts and mementoes of the TITANIC and related history gathered by the society over the years, and the second goal is to obtain photographs of the TITANIC in her present locale. Both are difficult dreams to attain as both require high finances that the society can ill-afford at this time despite the growth of the club in its short existence. Perhaps with expanded membership in the future and (hopefully) grants from other institutions and/or individuals, such dreams will one day be realized.

The TITANIC COMMUTATOR, official THS publication, will continue to print items of interest and 1976 will begin with another tribute to the OLYMPIC, sister-ship of the TITANIC. This present December 1975 issue contains material related to the GEORGIC and BRITANNIC, ships that sailed under the White Star Line burgee and it is thanks to THS Active Member, Charles Haas, who did some extensive research on these two ships, that we present this article. Other liners of the White Star Line will be featured in years to come, but the main interest, TITANIC and OLYMPIC will continue to be accented in the TITANIC COMMUTATOR.

Regarding future meetings of the society, much consideration was given to a possible convention in 1976, but THS officers came to the general conclusion that this Bi-Centennial year and its many celebrations throughout the country might hinder a meeting for our own organization. It is very probable that 1977 will be the year for the THS convention and by that time, perhaps the club will have reached beyond the 2,000-member mark. Nothing seems impossible in the TITANIC HISTORICAL SOCIETY with so many dedicated members who continue to "Remember The TITANIC!!"

"The Economy as Titanic,"
The New York Times

LESTER C. THUROW (1938–)
Economist, Journalist
August 24, 1980

As our economic ship of state slowly sinks into the briny deep, the bridge is manned by a captain, President Carter, who has led it into disaster. Down in the engine room a would-be captain, Ronald Reagan, is planning to restart the ship's hot engine by throwing economic gasoline on it. Back on the deck another would-be captain, John B. Anderson, is trying to still the economic gales with old sea tales of 50-cent gasoline taxes.

Look at what has happened to the ship since Mr. Carter took command. Between the first quarter of 1977 and the second quarter of 1980, the annual rate of inflation has risen from 6 to 10 percent; unemployment was 7.4 percent and falling, now it is 7.8 percent and rising; the gross national product was growing, but is now falling at a record 9 percent pace; productivity, measured in output per hour of work, was slowly rising, but is now falling at a 3 percent rate. These are the dry statistics of a first-class economic disaster.

In the naval traditions in which the President was educated, the captain of a ship that had incurred a disaster of this magnitude would be relieved of his command unless it could be shown that the blame lay entirely with unforeseeable bad luck and not with bad judgment. But it is clear that the captain and his appointed executive officer, Chairman Paul A. Volcker at the Federal Reserve Board, panicked at the beginning of 1980 and shut down the economy's engines when a faulty gauge, the consumer price index, showed that inflation was up to 17 percent.

If inflation had really reached 17 percent, one could understand the captain's decision to throw two million crew members into the seas of unemployment, but all of Washington knows that the consumer price index exaggerates inflation because of the way in which it handles housing and mortgage interest rates. The real rate of inflation was never 17 percent. The price index for the entire economy, the G.N.P. implicit price deflator, rose from an 8.2 percent rate in the last six months of 1979 to a 9.1 percent rate in the first three months of 1980.

Instead of calming the passengers and crew, the President compounded the panic with his quick budget reversals and tight monetary policies. And if current forecasts are right, those two million newly unemployed people are not going to solve the inflation problem. A leading economic forecasting firm, Data Resources, projects that the 9 percent inflation rate of 1979 will continue through 1980 and 1981.

Meanwhile down in the engine room Mr. Reagan plans to cure America's problems with a 30 percent personal income tax cut over the next three years and a speed-up in corporation depreciation allowances that will essentially halve the corporate income tax. This $140 billion tax cut is to be combined with a very large, but unspecified, increase in the $60 billion in extra defense spending already scheduled by Mr. Carter. While the economy certainly needs some highly targeted investment stimulus to get its engines going again, it just as certainly cannot take anything like this amount of economic stimulus without exploding.

The "tax cuts cure everything" philosophy is essentially the same as that adopted by Margaret Thatcher and the British Conservative Party. In Britain this strategy has doubled the rate of both unemployment and inflation without any positive effect on productivity. There is every reason to expect the same result here. America's economic problems are a lot more complicated than a lack of personal initiative caused by high taxation.

As for Mr. Anderson, never has so little intellectual gasoline taken a Presidential candidate so far. One can wonder about the mythological character of his 50-cent-per-gallon gasoline tax when Congress cannot digest a mere 10-cent gas tax. Or one can understand that a really effective gasoline tax would have to be in the $2- to $3-per-gallon range like those already adopted by most European countries. But a gasoline tax is not going to save the American economy. Energy is just one of our many problems.

While the public alternates between the inflation and unemployment as its main economic problem, the real problem is falling productivity. So long as productivity is falling, the country will be in the midst of an economic disaster even if it eliminates both inflation and unemployment. When productivity falls, real standards of living must fall; there is simply less output to be divided among Americans. Productivity growth is now down almost 3 percent below its 1978 peak and back to the level of 1976. As a consequence, real per capita standards of living have also fallen almost 3 percent.

The President is about to arrive with a new set of navigational directions to rechart the economy, but these new directions are simply arriving too close to an election to be taken seriously as an economic program rather than as a re-election gimmick.

With falling real incomes for the average middle-class household—one with an annual income of $18,000—it would be surprising if the voters did not want to cut Government expenditures for those less fortunate than themselves. With declining real income, a rational economic budgeter would want to cut some of those expenditures called taxes. To restore middle-class altruism and concern for the poor, it is going to be necessary to restore rising middle-class incomes. This means growth in productivity. Without it, cries of "jobs, jobs, jobs" aren't going to be answered.

"Bon Voyage," The Washington Post

LOU CANNON (1933–)
Columnist, Biographer
December 8, 1986

Trying to find the silver lining in the clouds gathering over the Reagan presidency, a White House official declared last week, "This is one of the best years the president has ever had, excepting Iran."

This assessment by Dennis Thomas, a principal deputy to White House chief of staff Donald T. Regan, was eerily reminiscent of a similar formulation by President Richard M. Nixon's press secretary, Ronald L. Ziegler, during the Watergate scandal. Summing up Nixon's achievements, Ziegler told me, "We had a good year, except for Watergate."

Understandably, Ziegler was annoyed when I wrote that his contention was comparable to saying that the Titanic had a good voyage, except for the iceberg. But Ziegler had a stronger case than the present occupants of the White House, particularly if the definition of a "good year" includes foreign policy.

Watergate demonstrated, as Elliot L. Richardson has said, that the Nixon presidency was "rotten at the core." The Iran arms scandal, even before the revelation that the proceeds from this incredible enterprise were diverted to aid the Nicaraguan contras, exposes some of Reagan's most cherished pretensions about foreign policy and presidential management.

In terms of management, the pretension is that Reagan has succeeded as president because he has a view of the "big picture" happily uncluttered by operational details. Unfortunately, Reagan's disenchantment with detail long ago became an alibi for his disengagement from operational substance.

Reagan rarely asks questions or reads anything more complicated than a condensed briefing summary or an adventure novel. The limitations of this approach have been compounded in the second term by Regan, who has effectively isolated the president from confrontations where Reagan's intuition might have rescued him.

A management style almost designed to keep the president ill-informed has reinforced a pretension in foreign policy that might have taken as its text the Reagan aphorism that "there are simple answers— just not easy ones." As California governor, Reagan dropped this line from his speeches at the behest of aides, but it remained an animating principle of his political approach and helped elect him president in 1980.

At a time when American hostages were held in the U.S. Embassy in Tehran and President Jimmy Carter was their surrogate political captive in Washington, something was quite appealing about Reagan's naive view that the world would change if he were elected and reasserted national verities. After his election, Reagan ratified the confidence of his countrymen by welcoming the released hostages and promising "swift and effective retribution" for future hostage-taking.

"We hear it said that we live in an era of limit to our powers," Reagan said then, demonstrating his belief in the simple nature of governance. "Well, let it also be understood that there are limits to our patience."

Even greater were the limitations of Reagan's understanding. He began by believing that "terrorists," as he then described the government of Iran, could be restrained by warnings. He learned, after many terrorist acts and the deaths of more than 200 Marines in Lebanon, that warnings did not suffice. He swayed back and forth between conflicting recommendations of advisers, first renouncing antiterrorist retaliation that killed civilians as terrorist attacks in their own right but eventually endorsing a bombing raid on Libya in which civilians were among the principal victims.

Despite the contradictions and casualties, Reagan appeared in the sixth year of his presidency to have made headway in his struggle against terrorism. The symbol of his progress was a reluctant consensus among European allies, who had begun to take steps against terrorist states long advocated by Reagan and Secretary of State George P. Shultz.

This fragile consensus was shattered beyond repair by the clandestine arms sales to Iran, a deal whose shadowy beginnings occurred as Reagan was calling Iran a member of "a confederation of terrorist states" that included Nicaragua, Libya, Cuba and North Korea. Reagan's defense of this deal suggests that he did not take his own policy seriously, let alone his promises to the freed hostages. The Titanic had a terrific voyage, except for the iceberg.

Reaganism of the Week: In a Time magazine interview, the president said Lt. Col. Oliver L. North "is a national hero. My only criticism is that I wasn't told everything."

"Reagan's Scandal," Letter to the Editor,
The Los Angeles Times

PETER SIMMEL
March 17, 1987

When the President admitted in his television speech, "This happened on my watch," did he draw upon his Navy career in Hollywood or was he quoting the captain of the Titanic?

"Aboard the S.S. Clinton," *Editorial,*
The Boston Herald

June 29, 1994

In the latest rearrangement of the deck chairs, President Clinton has kicked his chief of staff, an Arkansas boyhood friend, upstairs and turned to his budget director to ride herd on the White House. But a new deck crew can't steer the ship away from the iceberg.

Remember, old Washington hand David Gergen was going to bring some perspective. Then old Washington hand Lloyd Cutler was going to add gravity and sagacity. They probably did—see any difference?

The latest old Washington hand riding to the rescue is Leon Panetta, up to now budget director, who will take over from chief of staff Mack McLarty. Pardon our yawn.

Only the president is responsible for how the White House works.

John Sununu, chief of staff to President Bush, alienated everyone with his bullying and was tossed over the side. His replacement by old smoothie Sam Skinner didn't bring a dime's worth of help to the Bush presidency.

McLarty has been described as a doorkeeper. That's what the president wanted. He has been his own chief of staff, running large endless meetings and tolerating several different "power centers" (his wife, his campaign advisers, the vice president) whose members have been able to dive into any issue. We don't think it will matter much if the meetings now break up on time. It's the president's policies that count, and the voters know that.

Zig-zagging over Haiti, China, Bosnia and North Korea can't be blamed on who chaired the meetings or how many people came. It didn't matter which power center gave us a Rube Goldberg health care proposal that aroused fears of a bumbling bureaucracy, and whose major features won practically no support in Congress. Don't worry about who's got deck duty. What counts is the course of the ship.

"The Selling of the Titanic,"
The Titanic Commutator

EDWARD S. KAMUDA (1939–)
Founder, Titanic Historical Society
February 1996

During November and early December, we received telephone calls and letters about bits of "rare" *Titanic* coal being sold. That announcement appeared in newspapers, radio and television. The media often publicizes the controversial or outrageous to grab attention and the coal is certainly in that category.

That degradation reminded us that there seems to be nothing considered too shameless or perverse to be made the subject of an article or story. When General Colin Powell announced he would not run for the presidency in 1996, he was asked to describe in the broadest terms the message he would have liked to bring to the American people as a candidate for President. His reply was that he would like "to restore a sense of shame in society."

That O. J. Simpson was contemplating selling autographed photos of his Bronco while he purportedly had a pistol in his mouth while traveling down a Los Angeles freeway, or that serial killers Ted Bundy and Jeffrey Dahmer tee-shirts are sold and his refrigerator was going to be auctioned shows how low we have sunk. The coal, broken down from two tons retrieved and being sold by RMS Titanic Inc. came from a graveyard. That they seek publicity for this debasement, even buying advertising and with feigned reverence naming the purchaser a "Conservator" (of the *Titanic?* . . . coal that is millions of years old!) is another reflection of the society we've created—one in which aberrance and irresponsibility is applauded, and style beats out substance every time. After all, there is no money to be made in being responsible.

These are the people that in 1987, 1993, and 1994 brought up thousands of items from the wrecksite of the *Titanic.* Evidently that is not enough and now they are hawking coal. Greed and tastelessness know no bounds.

Ever since the first artifact had been wrested from the wreck of the S.S. *Titanic,* it had been assumed by a gullible public that the salvors' intentions were only to "preserve the artifacts for education and for history." Even with assurances given there were reservations expressed by some when a portion of these items were going to be put on display at the National Maritime Museum in Greenwich, England. Prior to that opening in October, 1994, just several months earlier that year, Arnie Geller of RMS Titanic Inc. stated in the A&E/Greystone Production *Titanic, The Legend Lives On,* "It doesn't seem to fit quite right if it's only 82 years ago, so we have made a conscious decision to stay away from the ship itself with respect to any recovery work and confine it to the debris field." Indeed, *The Guardian* in its January 31, 1994 edition stated, "The Museum . . . also welcomed the company's undertaking that ' . . . material (taken from the *Titanic*) will never be sold or otherwise dispersed and will be kept together in a permanent display after the completion of the tour exhibition . . . ' " At the same time as the exhibit opened, company officials from RMS Titanic Inc. and others involved held a secret meeting—a Titanic Advisory Board, where the agenda included plans for cutting tools to be made to go inside the wreck. So much for one's word of " . . . a conscious decision to stay away from the ship itself . . ."!

These are the same people who sent out a press release stating there was a large explosion from a coal fire in the *Titanic* that might have sunk the ship. The 1912 inquiries answered these questions to the contrary. These are the same people who sent out a press release that for publicity purposes appeared to give (then took away) a pocket watch claimed to have belonged to *Titanic* survivor Edith Brown Haisman's father who died in the disaster. 1912 interviews of Mrs. Brown tell an entirely contradictory story. However, it was clever public relations to use an elderly lady's emotions as a promotion. Another *Titanic* survivor, Miss Beatrice Sandström was also taken advantage of—a remark attributed to her about finding her lost suitcase at the wrecksite was used in press reports when *Titanic* artifacts were brought to Norfolk, Virginia, suggesting she did not mind the efforts. Her friend's letter in this issue sets things straight. The announcement, however disingenuous, served its purpose by leaving the other impression. The latest in their string of press releases says the ship is deteriorating, like the sky is falling—let's manufacture a "crisis" so the plundering can be justified. However, they brought up fragile personal items from the dead made of paper and cloth. Dr. Ballard's* expeditions showed most of the destruction occurred at the time of the sinking and shortly afterwards when marine organisms ate most of the soft material. RMS Titanic Inc. continues to promote the "deterioration" line relying on an ignorant public. Dr. Ballard said, "He (George Tulloch, president of RMS Titanic Inc.) promised that they would only pick the debris field, yet their Maritime Museum exhibition included the ship's mast light. Photos from 1986 clearly show it attached to the ship." The forward mast and crow's nest were also damaged due to the salvagers ripping the telephone from it. It was intact in Ballard's 1986 expedition photos.

It is ironic that when the T.H.S., P.S.E.A. and others spoke out against salvage because it is a gravesite, suggesting the remains of the dead are still with the *Titanic*, Tulloch dismissed the notion, "No bodies have yet to be found." However, when a Hollywood-based film unit recently made dives photographing the wreck's interior, Tulloch, with stunning hypocrisy conveniently about-faced stating in a Los Angeles reporter's piece, "This is very distressing! The ship contains the remains of many passengers and this is a historical site! I cannot see how (they) could have done this without causing damage!" (Underlined emphasis is mine.)

Dr. Ballard's comments in the *New York Post*, November 9, 1995, on the sale of two tons of coal, enough for 400,000 golf-ball-sized macabre souvenirs, "The whole thing is tacky. George Tulloch is not a historian, archaeologist or scientist. This is blatant commercialization on the death of a lot of people." The article had remarks from other critics who noted Tulloch's "just in time for the holidays sale" is nothing more than "graverobbing." In the same piece, Tulloch was quoted, "For only $25, it's better than a tee-shirt!"

The selling and promotion is one more example of the glorifica-

---

*Robert Ballard led the expedition that found the wreck of the *Titanic* in 1985.

tion of the lowest common denominator. When peddling coal from a graveyard is acceptable to the public and can be dismissed or rationalized, after all, it's only a small matter—the larger picture has been lost because there is a greater principle. General Colin Powell's hope "to restore a sense of shame in society" is a reminder of how standards of decency have declined. We must all start to take responsibility even in small ways. You can begin changing that direction by deciding not to support graverobbing with your money.

"Titanic Problems Dog Clinton,"
The San Francisco Examiner

CHRISTOPHER MATTHEWS (1945–)
Journalist, Author, Television Personality
April 10, 1997

The Titanic did not sink, it turns out, the way we thought.

It wasn't a giant gash that brought that great ship down in 1912 after its midnight encounter with the iceberg but a series of small cuts that, had they been made separately, the British liner might have survived. The pressure of the North Atlantic did the rest, scientists believe, blasting 39,000 tons of icy water through the perforated hull like a fire hose into a can.

For a re-enactment of that celebrated night to remember, watch closely at what's happening to the ship of state. It's not some giant gash that's causing Bill Clinton's second term presidency to take on water but, like the unsinkable Titanic, a series of cuts.

The effect has been the same. To contain political damage from each new mini-scandal, the Clinton crew seals off one watertight compartment after another. Eventually, the bow sinks so low in the water that the icy sea comes crashing over the bulkheads.

This has been the story here in Washington since the pre-election scandal over foreign campaign money. Voters intending to vote Democratic for Congress went to the polls awash with fishy stories of Buddhist nuns whipping off $5,000 checks, of an Indonesian gardener giving the DNC a hundred times that amount.

The result: The Republicans kept control of the Congress and the subpoena power that comes with it. Instead of facing a second term allied with a Democratic-led Congress, Clinton faces a hostile Capitol Hill that demands he take the heat on both entitlement reform and any campaign irregularities that might be uncovered.

Other compartments were doomed to flood as one small embarrassment leaked into another. The foreign money story led to an expose by Watergate sleuth Bob Woodward about Beijing's attempt to buy political influence here.

Word that the Indonesia-based Lippo Corporation had given money to the Democrats led to word it had given Clinton pal Webb Hubbell a $100,000 job after he was forced to quit the Justice Department over an Arkansas billing dispute.

The focus on Hubbell exposed other cases of White House generosity toward Hillary Clinton's old law partner. The attention to hush money has raised questions about how Filegate figure Craig Livingstone is financing his legal defense.

As with the Titanic, none of these scandals by itself has caused mortal damage to Clinton, not on the surface. His standing in the opinion polls remains high. Nor would any one of the problems pose a long-term threat to Bill Clinton's presidency.

Yet, taken together—Whitewater, Travelgate, Filegate, the foreign campaign dollars, abuse of the Lincoln Bedroom, dialing for dollars by Vice President Al Gore on federal property, the coddling of Hubbell—have given Clinton's critics, including those in the press, their opportunity.

Like the North Atlantic of 85 years ago, the forces of Clinton's doom have seized their opportunity. While things still look fine above deck, too many of the compartments are taking water and the engine room is flooding.

Two months ago, the president might have taken the lead on Medicare and the Mideast. Today, he stands nervously on the bridge awaiting the latest damage report. If he does not get control of events, that is where historians will someday find him.

"The Year the Warning Lights Flashed On,"
Life

Timothy Ferris (1944–)
Journalist, Author, College Professor, Television and Radio Personality
January 1987

The first alert came with the explosion of the space shuttle *Challenger* against a clear blue Florida sky on January 28. Then on April 26 the pyrotechnic meltdown of the Chernobyl-4 nuclear reactor lit up the predawn skies of the Soviet Ukraine. And then, while investigators were sorting through the sea-wracked remains of *Challenger* and bull-dozers were burying the Chernobyl reactor in a concrete and plastic crypt, three men aboard the titanium mini-submarine *Alvin*—itself a technical wonder—descended 12,500 feet beneath the surface of the North Atlantic to make the first detailed photographs of that timeless symbol of technological hubris, the *Titanic.*

The message could not have been more forceful had the moving finger that interrupted King Belshazzar's banquet reappeared to write anew of our being weighed in the balance. The time had come to take a hard, fresh look at the growing dependency of fallible man upon dangerous machinery.

Though separated by gulfs of space and time, the three calamities share a common theme. In each case, skilled professionals, ignoring conspicuous warnings of the dangers involved, pushed the machinery they controlled beyond its limits. In each case, they appear to have done so because they had become so enthralled by the sheer splendor of the technology at their command that they neglected its limitations, putting their trust in an image of mechanical perfection rather than in a less perfect reality. And, in each case, the results were lethal. The lesson of the warning lights is that blind faith in technology can kill.

In an age of nuclear arms, we ignore that warning at our peril. Today we all live with—indeed, *in*—a gigantic war machine, built to deter aggression but capable of wreaking greater destruction than human civilization can be expected to endure. To push *this* machine too far would be to make a mistake from which there might well be no appeal. Our destiny would prove to have been augured not by glistening visions of fusion reactors and space stations, but by the scorched wreckage of the *Challenger*, the radioactive tomb of Chernobyl-4 and the rusting hulk of the *Titanic*—which was a world in itself, full of laughter and music, until the hour that human error plunged it into darkness.

"Human error" was the cause assigned to the Chernobyl meltdown by the Soviet State Committee on the Utilization of Atomic Energy, in its official report on the accident. The report is unusually candid and searching by Soviet standards, and its verdict seems just— if we keep in mind that the errors had been accumulating for years and were the fault of many more humans than just those who happened to be in the plant on the night of April 26.

The trouble with Reactor Number Four at the Chernobyl Nuclear Power Plant was not that it wasn't good enough, but that it was so good its operators thought of it as nearly foolproof. No hulking relic of Stalinist engineering, Chernobyl-4 was less than three years old—a powerful (six gigawatt) computer-controlled monument to modern technology that sported as good a safety record as any nuclear plant in the U.S.S.R. Chernobyl is in the countryside north of Kiev, but so unstinting is the faith of Soviet officials in the reliability of their reactors that they have situated others in the suburbs of major cities, where they could supply not only electricity but also steam heat for nearby office buildings and apartment houses. This frightening practice was justified by proclaiming that the reactors were too well designed to fail. After the Three Mile Island accident in 1979, the president of the Soviet Academy of Sciences was quick to offer assurances that it couldn't happen there. Soviet nuclear power plants, he said, "can be built in the middle of residential areas because they are absolutely safe."

It was in a comparably Panglossian frame of mind that the operators of Chernobyl-4 drove their reactor past the breaking point. Ironically enough, the disaster came during a series of tests to find improved ways of dealing with an emergency. Specifically, the plant technicians wanted to learn whether a freewheeling turbine could be used to power emergency equipment should the reactor malfunction and have to be shut down. To conduct the tests, they disabled various safety systems and throttled back the reactor to only 7 percent of full power, violating six successive sets of plant operating rules in all.

Running at such a low level, the reactor became as unstable as a bicycle at walking speed. Suddenly the power surged tenfold, turning the core white hot. A foreman pressed a button to stop the chain reaction by dropping control rods into the core, but by then it was too late. The core had already boiled the cooling water surrounding it into steam, and the steam promptly blew the roof off the plant. The reactor's 1,661 channels of nuclear fuel acted like giant Roman candles, blasting radioactive matter into the air and lighting up the night sky. Burning debris fell back onto the roof of the machine room, starting 30 separate fires. Firemen fought the flames for days in an environment so radioactively "hot" that some had to be relieved after only one minute of exposure.

Thirty-one persons at the site died outright, and more than 20,000 Europeans and Soviets are expected to contract radiation-induced cancers from Chernobyl over the course of the next 70 years. One hundred thirty-five thousand people were evacuated from the area, many never to return home again. The radioactive plume contaminated lettuce in Italy, milk in Poland and the mosses fed upon by reindeer in Lapland. The reactor itself was buried under 5,000 tons of lead, dolomite, clay and sand, and still continued to leak radiation. Bulldozers driven by astronautlike figures in white radiation suits stripped acres of contaminated topsoil, and paving trucks coated the denuded land with a thick skin of liquid plastic. Entombed in concrete, hazardous in perpetuity, Chernobyl-4 stands as an enduring monument to the worst nuclear accident in history.

Yet Soviet officials showed little immediate sign of having learned much from the accident. A Soviet delegate to a Vienna conference of the International Atomic Energy Agency in August asserted that his government, having taken steps to improve training programs for nuclear plant operators, could "guarantee" that another meltdown would never occur.

American nuclear power advocates, for their part, emphasized that most reactors in the U.S. have containment buildings designed to prevent radioactive material from being vented into the atmosphere in an accident. But containment buildings are not perfect. A report released last September by two nuclear power specialists, Robert D. Pollard and

Daniel F. Ford, concluded that the rubber O-rings used as seals in containment buildings in American reactors can fail under the high temperature and pressure of a nuclear fire, permitting radiation to escape. The Pollard-Ford report cited 62 instances of O-ring failure in American reactors since 1975.

It was, of course, an O-ring failure that doomed the space shuttle *Challenger*. But here, as at Chernobyl, the root cause of the accident had less to do with technology than with the failure of human beings to appreciate its limitations. NASA had known for years that O-rings on the shuttle's solid rocket boosters were vulnerable to failure in cold weather. O-rings on the spent rockets recovered from previous shuttle flights had shown signs of erosion on every mission launched in temperatures below 61°F. One engineer at Morton Thiokol, the builders of the solid rocket boosters, had cautioned NASA that O-ring failure could result in "a catastrophe of the highest order—loss of human life," while another had complained of the problem in a memo that began with "HELP!" and ended with "This is a red flag." On the morning of the launch, Thiokol reminded NASA that the rings were not certified safe below 50°F. The temperature on the launchpad at the time was 36°. But the engineers were overruled by management, and *Challenger* was launched at 11:38 A.M. from a tower festooned with icicles. An O-ring on the right booster failed at once, permitting a jet of hot vapor from inside the rocket to lap like a blowtorch against the spacecraft's tank of liquid fuel. The flame burned through the tank 73 seconds later, and the craft exploded, killing the five men and two women aboard and leaving the American space program in a shambles.

At hearings conducted by the presidential commission investigating the crash, the American public learned that NASA managers, thought to occupy the pinnacle of high-tech expertise, had been lulled into overconfidence. They underestimated the O-ring threat, said the commission, "partly because of their own well-nurtured image of the program." Former astronaut Wally Schirra put it more succinctly: "NASA," he said, "got caught reading its own notices."

The seeds of this fatal confusion of image with reality had been planted at the very inception of the shuttle program, when NASA officials, fearful that they could not otherwise obtain congressional funding, mounted an energetic public relations campaign that depicted the shuttle as all things for all people. The agency promised that the shuttle would loft scientific payloads into orbit, provide the Pentagon with access to the "high ground" of space, offer an efficient, economical means of launching communications satellites and turn a profit in the bargain. The shuttle's promoters viewed the future through glasses as rosy as those worn by the Soviet engineers who employed nuclear power to steam-heat the suburbs of Gorky and Odessa. Life imitated PR: The first space shuttle was named the *Enterprise,* after the spaceship in the television series *Star Trek.*

The real shuttle, however, could no more fly at a profit or meet its flight-a-fortnight launch schedule than it could speed Mr. Spock to the stars. As costs rose and delays multiplied, NASA cut back crew training, cannibalized parts from its own spacecraft and deferred spending a half billion dollars on safety. Faced with a widening disparity between the unpleasant facts and the shuttle's glistening public relations image, NASA officials increasingly chose to believe in the image—which, in turn, drifted ever further from reality. The odds of a fatal shuttle crash were variously estimated at one in a hundred to one in a hundred thousand; the *Challenger* mission, the program's 25th, proved all the odds too high.

The justification for NASA's trust in its flawed spacecraft came down to the fact that it hadn't blown up yet: As at Chernobyl, the accumulation of an impressive safety record in the past came to be taken as a guarantee that nothing could go wrong in the future. "The argument that the same risk was flown before without failure is often accepted as an argument for the safety of accepting it again," noted Richard Feynman, the Nobel Prize-winning physicist who served on the presidential commission. But, Feynman added, "when playing Russian roulette, the fact that the first shot got off safely is little comfort for the next."

It was Feynman, a gifted experimenter with a distaste for cant, who cut through reams of bureaucratic obfuscation on the O-ring question by simply immersing a piece of O-ring material in a pitcher of ice water during a break in the committee hearings and noting that it grew brittle. The trouble with NASA's believing its own press clippings, Feynman noted, was that nature had not read them. "Reality must take precedence over public relations," he concluded, "for nature cannot be fooled."

The *Titanic* departed on her maiden voyage in 1912 buoyed by a similarly misplaced faith in modern technology. Here, too, the blandishments of publicity worked to deceive even the experts. The press described the *Titanic* as "practically unsinkable," and the owners and operators of the ship came to believe it. But the real ship behind the image of invulnerability was neither unsinkable nor even particularly safe. The *Titanic*'s much touted water-tight compartments extended only 10 feet above the waterline, and it carried enough lifeboats for only a fraction of its passengers and crew.

Cautions against this cavalier approach to safety had been voiced for years. Those unacquainted with the technical details needed only to have read Morgan Robertson's 1898 novel *Futility*, which envisioned a luxurious and "unsinkable" liner striking an iceberg in the North Atlantic on a cold April night and sinking with insufficient lifeboats aboard to save her rich and famous passengers. Robertson's fictitious liner, 800 feet long and the largest ever built, was called the *Titan.*

The *Titanic*'s size, even longer, was itself an exercise in image-building. J. P. Morgan had put together a trust to monopolize the North Atlantic passenger trade. As a publicity ploy, he approved a plan to build the largest ship in the world. But the ship's bulk misled even its creators. As Walter Lord, the author of *A Night to Remember,* writes in his new book, *The Night Lives On,* "The owners were lulled into complacency . . . because the ship *looked* so safe. Her huge bulk, her tiers of decks rising one atop the other, her twenty-nine boilers, her luxurious fittings—all seemed to spell 'permanence.'

"The appearance of safety," Lord concludes, "was mistaken for safety itself."

Ship's masters in those days made it a practice to proceed at cruising speed even in winter, relying upon their sharp-eyed lookouts to spot icebergs in time to slow down and steer around them. Captain Edward J. Smith, a veteran master making what he intended to be his retirement crossing, kept the *Titanic* steaming at 22 knots even after his wireless operators had passed along a half dozen radio messages from ships ahead warning of icebergs. But the *Titanic* was too massive to dodge icebergs as smaller ships could. At cruising speed she was, so to speak, outdriving her headlights.

At 11:40 P.M. on Sunday, April 14, the lookout phoned down to the bridge, "Iceberg dead ahead." The wheel was spun hard to starboard and the engines were reversed, but the *Titanic* was slow to respond. It struck the iceberg just aft of the starboard bow and sank in less than three hours.

The *Titanic's* final hour produced many tales of valor—women chose to perish rather than leave their husbands, and men dying in the icy water urged those in the lifeboats to row away rather than risk being swamped. But that sort of gallantry was soon to expire on the barbed wire of the First World War, when the machinery of human slaughter rendered courage almost irrelevant. "All our lauded technological progress," Albert Einstein wrote sadly in 1917, has become "like the axe in the hand of a pathological criminal."

Today the machinery of war has grown to proportions that only Einstein and a few other visionaries could have foreseen. We have all become passengers on the dark ship of nuclear deterrence, our fate dependent upon the proposition that it will never fail.

But never is a long time, and the war machine is not infallible. In 1980 B-52s at 33 air bases were warmed up for takeoff when the failure of a 46-cent computer chip resulted in a spurious warning of a Soviet missile attack. Soon after its installation in 1960, a U.S. early warning radar system in Greenland picked up hundreds of "incoming missiles" that turned out to be craters on the rising moon. When a surprise test of the White House emergency evacuation system was conducted by an aide to Jimmy Carter in 1977, the helicopter that was supposed to save the President from nuclear attack took much too long to arrive and was nearly shot down by the Secret Service.

Its frailties notwithstanding, we have come to rely on the war machine. The longer we live with it, the more difficult it is to imagine the world without it. We become transfixed, like deer staring into the headlights of an oncoming car. The high technology of defense can be "sweet," as physicist Edward Teller likes to say. There is a terrible beauty in a computer on a Navy destroyer discerning the identity of a submerged submarine and even the name of its captain from nothing more than the distant whirr of its motors, or in a ballistic missile gliding silently through space, consulting the crystal ball of its inertial guidance system while it keeps an eye on the star Canopus, slewing itself into position to dispatch a dozen conical, flat-black nuclear warheads toward targets far below. Contemplating these horrific wonders year after year, we become more machinelike ourselves. The stewardship of human affairs, however, remains the responsibility of human beings and can no more be attained by imitating machines than by abdicating to them.

At the apex of blind faith in defense technology stands the Strategic Defense Initiative—SDI, or Star Wars, President Reagan's mandate to find a way of destroying enemy warheads from space before they can reach American soil. Though often described as an impervious, invulnerable robot, an SDI system actually could be expected to knock out only a portion of the incoming warheads. Suppose, for example, that the Soviets fired a salvo of 10,000 warheads at the U.S. According to the most optimistic predictions of SDI proponents, if the system functioned ideally—on the first try, without ever having been tested in battle—it might succeed in destroying as many as 90 percent of the warheads, leaving 10 percent to hit their targets. Although the prospect of 1,000 nuclear bombs striking North America is not a happy one— it would almost certainly spell the end of our civilization—presumably it would be preferable to 10,000, even if few were left alive to appreciate the difference.

There is, however, another way to attain the same degree of security. It is for both sides to reduce their arsenals to 10 percent of their present size, through verifiable arms reduction treaties. This would accomplish the avowed mission of SDI while saving the U.S. up to one trillion dollars. But the President wants the SDI "shield." The implication appears to be that while arms treaties are merely human and therefore fallible, SDI can be trusted because SDI is high tech.

Those who are the most familiar with defense technology tend also to be the most skeptical about the hope that any such purely technological "fix" can save us from ourselves. What Albert Einstein and Bertrand Russell wrote of nuclear arms in 1954—that "the men who know most are the most gloomy"—remains true today, which is why 7,000 of America's leading scientists have pledged to refuse SDI funding.

Technological wonders like Chernobyl, *Challenger* and the *Titanic* are no more trustworthy than are the human beings who design and operate them. The gleaming machinery of strategic defense is imposing, to be sure, but it was built by people to address people's problems, and people can choose to dismantle it in favor of less dangerous alternatives. Einstein, who in the course of pure research into the nature of space and time unwittingly revealed the possibility of building nuclear weapons, understood better than most that these new engines of destruction only increased the need to search for humane rather than technological solutions to our problems. "We appeal," he and Russell wrote, "as human beings, to human beings: Remember your humanity and forget the rest. If you can do so, the way lies open to a new paradise; if you cannot, there lies before you the risk of universal death."

"Titanic Baby Found Alive!"
Weekly World News

REX WOLFE
June 22, 1993

A 10-month-old girl thought to have perished on the *Titanic* has been rescued from a life preserver in the North Atlantic—81 years after the ocean liner sank on its maiden voyage in 1912!

The discovery of the cold and confused but apparently healthy child comes just three years after *Titanic* survivors Winnie Coutts and Capt. E. J. Smith were found in the same area, leading experts to speculate that more passengers might be drifting aimlessly in the ocean, just waiting to be found.

"This story just won't go away," Dr. Malvin Iddleland, the famed maritime researcher, told newsmen in Oslo, Norway.

"I wish I could tell you what's happening out there in the North Atlantic, but frankly, it defies all logic.

"These aren't impostors we've found—these are people who boarded the *Titanic* in 1912 and should have drowned when it sank. As a serious scientist, I never thought I would hear myself say something like this.

"But in this particular part of the world, time seems to have lost its meaning.

"People who lived and died in 1912 are popping up like they were born yesterday.

"If that doesn't suggest that the *Titanic* and its passengers are trapped in some kind of a time warp, I don't know what does."

The discoveries of Miss Coutts in 1990, and Capt. Smith in 1991, made international headlines but were never really explained because the survivors aged rapidly and died just months after they were pulled from the sea.

In the latest incident, the crew of the Norwegian fishing boat *Hysstad-Sceter* spotted the girl clinging to a *Titanic*-issue life preserver about 220 miles southwest of Iceland on May 21.

Officials refuse to identify the child because she is a minor but they did release a photo taken by one of the crewmen of the *Hysstad-Sceter.*

And while Dr. Iddleland refused to elaborate, he claimed to have evidence to prove beyond a shadow of a doubt that she boarded the *Titanic* on its ill-fated voyage from Southampton, England, to New York in 1912.

The expert went on to say that the child is a patient of Dr. Jarle Haaland, who treated Miss Coutts and Capt. Smith before they died.

Information is sketchy. But Dr. Haaland confirmed that the girl was brought to the Saether Psychiatric Hospital in 1912 clothing and is much too young to understand anything that is happening to her.

"Passenger records from the *Titanic* indicate that the girl was 10 months old when she boarded ship with her mother and she obviously hasn't aged a day in all the years she's been missing," said Dr. Haaland. "Dealing with a patient this young is difficult because she can't speak and spends much of her time crying for her mother," he added.

"About all we can do is try to make the child comfortable in the time she has left. Winnie Coutts and Capt. Smith aged rapidly after they were rescued and we have reason to believe that this little girl will do the same.

"She may be a 10-month-old baby now, but that could change in a matter of weeks. By summer's end, our patient might not be a baby. She might be dying of old age.

"And there wouldn't be a damn thing we could do about it."

While Dr. Haaland continues to care for the child at Saether Hospital, Dr. Iddleland and other officials are searching *Titanic* records in hopes of finding something to "explain how the girl, as well as Capt. Smith and Miss Coutts, traveled into the future.

"We have alerted all ships in the area southwest of Iceland to keep an eye out for more survivors," he added. "For all we know, everyone who went down with the *Titanic* is still alive.

"I don't doubt anything anymore."

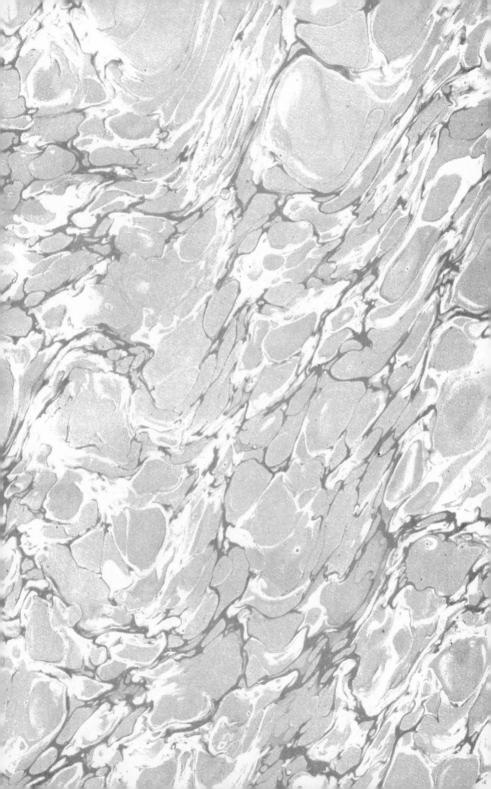

ADVERTISEMENTS

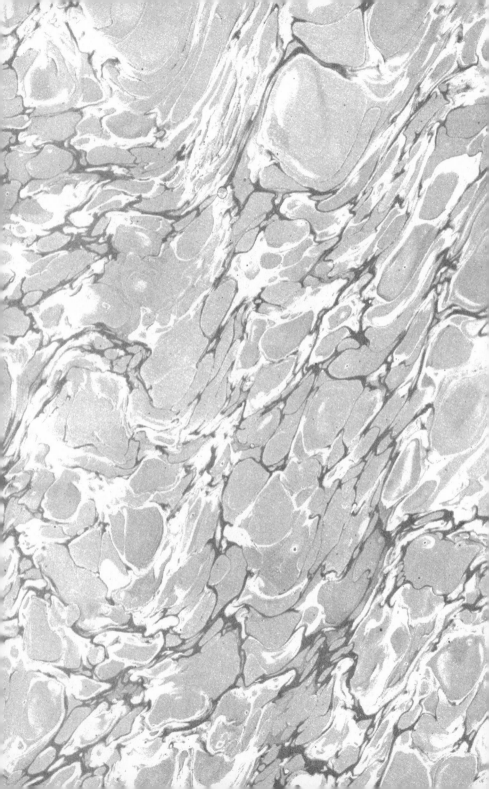

The Ocean's Greatest Disaster

May 1912

There has just been enacted the greatest ocean tragedy the world ever saw—the sinking of the gigantic ocean liner "Titanic" on her maiden voyage. The greatest ship ever built, with her precious cargo of human freight, went to the bottom of the ocean a thousand miles from shore amid a wilderness of icebergs. Multi-millionaires, authors, statesmen and immigrants share the same watery grave. Never before was there such an exhibition of heroism and chivalry. Picture the ship's musicians, ankle deep in the rising flood, trying to soften the anguish of the dying with strains of melody; husbands handing their wives into the life boats, while deluding them with false assurances of their own safety. Imagine that noble wife, choosing perhaps the happier part, and calmly refusing to go and remaining on the doomed ship by her husband's side. See the famous and brilliant men ungrudgingly standing aside for the poor peasant woman of the steerage. These heroes of real life bore themselves in a way that leaves the world richer and better for their having lived and died. Here, indeed, is a glorious glimpse of what man can do in a supreme moment. The whole world is afire with sympathy and sorrow, and every one who reads must have this permanent pictorial and descriptive record of the greatest ocean disaster in the world's history, the *Story of the Wreck of the Titanic.*

This great book, profuse with scores of wonderful illustrations, tells all the thrilling story, with personal accounts of heroic self-sacrifice, marvelous escapes, and terrible sufferings. It contains over three hundred and fifty pages of the most vivid descriptions that ever were penned by man. Every home in the nation must have this book. It is an inspiring example of heroism for the young, and will be treasured and cherished by the old. This is your opportunity to own a copy of *This Great "Memorial Edition" For Only $1.00.*

Want Ad

April 1912

THE TITANIC DISASTER; Authentic; Realistic; Heartrending; Bonanza for Agents; low price; big terms; outfit free. ZIEGLER CO.; Phila., Pa.

Mrs. Brown Refused to Sink

ADVERTISING COUNCIL
1955

Mrs. Brown
refused to sink

"Keep rowing or I'll toss you all overboard!"

The threat came from a redhead in corset and bloomers, with a Colt .45 lashed to her waist. And as the lifeboat marked *S. S. Titanic* lurched into the waves, she rowed too, rowed until her hands bled.

Mrs. Margaret Tobin Brown had come a long way to take charge of that crowded lifeboat. Once penniless, she now had millions. Once semi-illiterate, she now knew five languages. Once spurned by Denver society, she now hobnobbed with nobility.

But, as she said, "You can't wear the social register for water wings." Her $60,000 chinchilla cloak covered three children; her other outer garments she had given to elderly women. She swore, threatened, sang grand opera, joked—and she kept her boatload of wretched survivors going till rescue came.

Asked how she'd done it, she replied, "Typical Brown luck. I'm unsinkable." But it wasn't luck. It was pluck. And Americans have always had plenty of that smiling, hardy courage. When you come to think of it, that's one reason why our country's Savings Bonds rank among the world's finest investments.

For 160 million determined Americans stand behind those Bonds.

The surest way to protect your own security—and the nation's—is through United States Savings Bonds. Invest in them regularly—and hold on to them.

★   ★   ★

It's actually easy to save money—when you buy United States Series E Savings Bonds through the automatic Payroll Savings Plan where you work! You just sign an application at your pay office; after that your saving is done *for* you. And the Bonds you receive will pay you interest at the rate of 3% per year, compounded semiannually, for as long as 19 years and 8 months, if you wish! Sign up today! Or, if you're self-employed, invest in Bonds regularly where you bank.

Safe as America—
U.S. Savings Bonds